T0204524

One Hundred Frogs

TRANSLATIONS BY HIROAKI SATO

Poems of Princess Shikishi
Ten Japanese Poets
Spring & Asura: Poems of Kenji Miyazawa
Mutsuo Takahashi: Poems of a Penisist
Lilac Garden: Poems of Minoru Yoshioka
Howling at the Moon: Poems of Hagiwara Sakutarō
See You Soon: Poems of Taeko Tomioka
Chieko and Other Poems of Takamura Kōtarō

with Burton Watson
From the Country of Eight Islands: An Anthology of Japanese Poetry

ONE HUNDRED
FROGS

FROM RENGA TO
HAIKU TO ENGLISH

by Hiroaki Sato 1942–

WEATHERHILL
New York & Tokyo

Some portions originally prepared for this book were first printed in the *Chanoyu Quarterly* and *Frogpond*.

Most of the contributors' English haiku and renga first appeared in *Anthology 82*, *Bonsai*, *Brussels Sprout*, *Christian Science Monitor*, *Cicada*, *Dragonfly*, *Frogpond*, *Haiku*, *Haiku Highlights*, *Haiku Magazine*, *Haiku West*, *Light Footsteps*, *Listen to Light*, *Modern Haiku*, *A Roseliep Retrospective*, *Sailing Bones*, *Seer Ox*, *Shedding the River*, *Sky in My Legs*, *Step on the Rain*, *The Still Point*, *Tweed*, and *The Windless Orchard*.

Some of the quoted translations first appeared in *Chieko and Other Poems of Takamura Kōtarō*, translated by Hiroaki Sato (Honolulu: University Press of Hawaii, 1980); *The Complete Works of Chuang Tzu*, translated by Burton Watson (New York and London: Columbia University Press, 1968); *From the Country of Eight Islands*, translated by Hiroaki Sato and Burton Watson (Garden City, New York: Doubleday & Company; Seattle: University of Washington Press, 1981); *Japanese Linked Poetry*, Earl Miner (Princeton: Princeton University Press, 1979); and *Meng Ch'iu*, translated by Burton Watson (Tokyo: Kodansha International, 1979). All quotations are made with permission.

Credits for the monochrome photographs are due Idemitsu Art Gallery, Kadokawa Library, Kakie Library, Shōgakukan Publishing Co., and Shūeisha.

to Burton Watson

Contents

Preface   *ix*

Some Poetic Terms Used in This Book   *xiii*

Part One • From Renga to Haiku

1   The Early History of Renga   *3*

     General Rules   *18*

     Specific Rules   *29*

     Optional Rules   *34*

2   Courtly Elegance, Earthy Humor, and Poetry   *43*

3   Bashō and Poetry Writing as a Group Activity   *88*

     Renga at the Time of Bashō   *88*

     Renga Since the Time of Bashō   *106*

4   From Hokku to Haiku   *113*

5   Some Aspects of the Question,
     What Is a Haiku?   *126*

Part Two • Translating into English

6   Translating Hokku, Haiku, and Renga   *135*

7   One Hundred Frogs   *147*

Part Three • Composing in English

8   English Renga   *179*

    Two-Part Excerpts   *181*
    Full Sequences   *189*
        bronze shield, by Geoffrey O'Brien, Hiroaki
          Sato, and James Kirkup   *189*
        Rickshaw (or Buddha Comes to the West), Solo
          Renga by Cor van den Heuvel   *193*
        As the fog thickens, by Hiroaki Sato, Geraldine
          Little, and Marlene Wills   *195*
        In your panties, Solo Renga by Hiroaki Sato   *199*
        Past midsummer, by Michael O'Brien, Lindley
          Williams Hubbell, and Hiroaki Sato   *203*

9   English Haiku   *207*

        L. A. Davidson   *208*
        Elizabeth Searle Lamb   *210*
        Geraldine Little   *212*
        Raymond Roseliep   *213*
        Cor van den Heuvel   *216*
        Marlene Wills   *218*
        Virginia Brady Young   *221*

Epilogue, by Eleanor Wolff   *223*
Sources and Credits for
  One Hundred Frogs, I   *225*
Index   *231*

Illustrations appear following page 114

Preface

The principal forms of Japanese poetry developed in a remarkably genealogical way. First, the *tanka,* a poem of 31 syllables arranged in units of 5, 7, 5, 7, and 7 syllables, became dominant in the eighth century and went on to be adopted as the standard form of court poetry. Then came the *renga;* consisting of alternating 5-7-5– and 7-7–syllable parts, it grew out of the tendency of the tanka to break up into this same pattern. Popular as early as the tenth century, the renga acquired literary importance in the fourteenth century and remained supreme for the next several hundred years. Finally came the 5-7-5–syllable *hokku.* Originally the opening part of a renga sequence, the hokku in time became independent. Around the year 1900 the term hokku was displaced by the term *haiku.* Today, anywhere from three hundred thousand to one million people in Japan write poems in this 5-7-5–syllable form.

If genealogical development is one outstanding feature of Japanese poetry, group orientation in its composition is another. Tanka were often composed in or for a group of people—most notably in *uta-awase,* tanka matches, where tanka by different poets were judged in pairs. The group orientation of this form is also manifest in any of the twenty-one imperial anthologies of Japanese poetry. In these, tanka are classified into categories such as spring, summer, autumn, winter, love, and miscellaneous, and the pieces selected for each category are so arranged as to indicate temporal progession. Here the appropriateness of a given piece for a given place is of primary importance. Individual poems, and therefore individual poets, are subordinated to the design of a larger whole.

Group orientation found its ultimate expression in the renga, which in principle required the participation of two or more persons. As a sophisticated game for literate people, the renga engendered some distinctive features, such as the set roles of host, guest of honor (or "master"), and scribe, and the rules of composition partly governed by their relations. Also characteristic were the stress on enjoyment, readiness to collaborate, effort to maintain a common literary milieu, and attention given to etiquette. Its deliberate avoidance of linear narrative development, or the technique of "disjunctive linking," as Earl Miner put it, shows renga's origin as a contest of wit in a group, with each poet called upon to cap a statement in verse, rather than one poet creating a whole story. As might be expected, hokku also tended to be written in group settings. In Japan today this predilection for making poetry writing a group activity remains particularly strong among writers of traditional haiku and tanka.

In Part One of this book I try mainly to describe the renga form, with the focus on Matsuo Bashō (1644–94). This I do because this book began as a collection of English translations of Bashō's most famous hokku, *Furuike ya kawazu tobikomu mizu no oto*. When the opportunity arose to publish the collection in an expanded format, I felt it best to go back to the renga, of which the hokku form was born, to explain Bashō's poem. As recent books such as *Japanese Linked Poetry* (Princeton: Princeton University Press, 1979) and *The Monkey's Straw Raincoat and Other Poetry of the Bashō School* (Princeton: Princeton University Press, 1981) have shown, Bashō can be fully appreciated only as a renga poet, and his hokku, in the context of renga. Also, during my stint as president of the Haiku Society of America from 1979 to 1981, I was often asked, "What is a haiku?" This question apparently has a good deal to do with the Zen overtones ascribed to Bashō's hokku, the validity of which I have doubted. I hope to offer the description of renga here as my response to the question.

In Part Two I explain why I translate the way I do. This is followed by the collection mentioned above. I do not discuss the merits or demerits of the many attempts I have assembled; judgment of this kind is a matter of preference to a great extent, and the question is largely answered, I think, within the collection. In Part Three I give small samplings of renga and haiku in English. English haiku can be read in many books now, but I believe this is the first time English renga have been presented as they are here.

Following the publisher's request to "keep the footnotes to an absolute minimum," I decided to give none. It is difficult to go halfway in giving notes. I hope I have largely made up for this by transliterating most of the original poems and, when that is not done, by citing references wherever possible. Further, most of the unnamed sources are identifiable with relative ease, because they are limited in number and length. The exception to the annotational rule in this book is the first group of translations in chapter 7 for which a complete listing of sources is part of the game.

Among the books and articles in English that I read to write this book but did not cite by author's name or by title are "The Japanese Comic Linked-Verse Tradition," Howard S. Hibbett, *Harvard Journal of Asiatic Studies,* 23 (1960–61); "The Comic Tradition in Renga," Donald Keene, *Japan in the Muromachi Age,* edited by John Whitney Hall and Toyoda Takeshi (Berkeley: University of California Press, 1977); *Landscapes and Portraits,* Donald Keene (London: Secker and Warburg, 1972); *The Art of Chinese Poetry,* James J. Y. Liu (Chicago: University of Chicago Press, 1962); *The Japanese Tradition in British and American Literature,* Earl Miner (Princeton: Princeton University Press, 1956; reprinted in 1976 by Greenwood Press); *Sengai,* Daisetz T. Suzuki (Greenwich: New York Graphic Society, 1971); *Literary and Art Theories in Japan,* Makoto Ueda (Cleveland: The Press of Western Reserve University, 1967); and *Chinese Lyricism,* Burton Watson (New York and London: Columbia University Press, 1971).

In my essays all Japanese names are given in Japanese fashion: family name first, personal name second. This is not always so elsewhere, especially with Japanese authors who have published their books and articles in English. I follow those authors' practice and write my name in the Occidental way.

The pronunciation of Japanese is easy. There are five vowels, and each can be long or short; when long, it is indicated by a macron in transliteration, as in Bashō. The vowels are roughly pronounced as follows: *a,* as in f*a*ther; *e,* as in s*e*t; *i,* as in mach*i*ne; *o,* as in t*o*rt; and *u,* as in rh*u*barb. The consonants are more or less pronounced as in English, except that *ch* is always pronounced as in *ch*urch and *g* is always hard.

My friend Kyoko Selden sowed the seed of this book one day several years ago when she listed twenty translations of Bashō's hokku and asked if I could tell their authors. A larger list I then made lay dormant until Donald Richie remembered it and passed it on to Meredith Weatherby, who reacted positively. I first thank these three persons for their elegant turn of mind. I also thank L. A. Davidson, Elizabeth Searle Lamb, Geraldine Little, Raymond Roseliep, Cor van den Heuvel, Marlene Wills, and Virginia Brady Young for contributing their haiku and renga and for giving information on the history of the two forms in the United States; Liza Dalby, Fujii Misako, Hirata Takako, Itoi Michihiro, Koyanagi Reiko, and Yano Sumiko for obtaining books and articles hard to come by in New York City; Jonathan Chaves for providing scholarly information on Chinese linked poetry, *lien-chü,* and translating an example, *Gladdened by the Rain on the River Huai* by Su Shun-ch'in and Su Shun-yüan; and Robert Fagan, Kusama Junko, Nancy Rossiter, Burton Watson, and Eleanor Wolff for helping me improve the manuscript. Mr. Watson also graciously translated the verses and phrases originally in Chinese that are quoted here but do not appear in any of his books.

Some Poetic Terms Used in This Book

The following explanations are for quick reference. The definitions of the three most important terms—renga, hokku, and haiku—are brief because this book is primarily about them. In the essays the poetic terms are italicized, as a rule, only the first time they are used.

ageku (ending part): the last part, in 7-7 syllables, of a renga sequence.

daisan (the third): the third part, in 5-7-5 syllables, of a renga sequence.

fushimono (incorporated object): a word or image required to be incorporated in part or in the whole of a renga sequence.

haibun (haikai prose): prose written in a *haikai* spirit, often incorporating hokku.

haikai (humor): a term that originally meant "humor" but came to mean, in renga, the use of non-poetic diction and, still later, various conceits and transcendental attitudes.

haiku (haikai part): a modern term for hokku.

hokku (opening part): the initial part, in 5-7-5 syllables, of a renga sequence.

kasen (divine poet): a renga sequence consisting of thirty-six parts. The term derives from the old practice of designating thirty-six "divine poets."

kigo (seasonal word): a word or phrase indicating one of the four seasons; for example, *zansetsu* (remaining snow) indicates spring, and *momiji chiru* (maple leaves scatter), winter. The idea of having an object or a phenomenon represent a season was helped by the concept of *hon'i* (true import) that holds that any object or phenomenon essentially has a single attribute.

maeku (preceding part): part immediately preceding a link in a renga sequence.

maeku-zuke (linking to a preceding part): (1) composing a link or links to a *maeku*, and (2) the link or links so composed. This type of composition was mostly done independent of renga and eventually spawned the *senryū*.

renga (linked poetry): a sequential form of poetry that consists of two to a hundred alternating 5-7-5– and 7-7–syllable parts.

senryū (eponymous with Karai Senryū): 5-7-5–syllable form of poetry free of some of the requirements of the hokku.

tanka (short song): 5-7-5-7-7–syllable form of poetry.

tsukeai (linking together): composing a link in a renga sequence.

tsukeku (linked part): part composed to be linked to another.

waki, wakiku (accompanying part): the second part, in 7-7 syllables, of a renga sequence.

PART ONE
FROM RENGA TO HAIKU

~·~ CHAPTER ONE ~·~

The Early History of Renga

Matsuo Bashō (1644–94) is universally known as the greatest writer in surely one of the shortest poetic forms in the world, 5-7-5–syllable haiku. But Bashō earned his living and reputation in a longer, far more complicated form called renga, linked poetry, of which the haiku was originally no more than the opening part. A renga consists of two to a hundred alternating parts of 5-7-5 and 7-7 syllables, usually written by two or more persons, with the linking made in such a way that any two consecutive parts must make an intelligible whole, but three may not. It is collaborative poetry with "disjunctive linking." How this unique poetic form—for it is unique—evolved is the concern of this chapter.

First, let us look at two episodes showing how renga in its pristine form may have been composed. One is told by Minamoto no Toshiyori (1055–1129) in his treatise on poetry writing, *Zuinō* (Elemental Poetics):

"When Tamemasa was governor of Kawachi, one morning it snowed. Because he had nothing special to do, he closed the sliding paper doors on his side, gathered his servants, and was drinking sakè, when Minamoto no Shigeyuki [a noted poet] came by on his way elsewhere. Tamemasa was overjoyed and offered him sakè. When everyone was drunk, Shigeyuki pushed open the paper doors, looked out, and saw a snow-covered mountain, so he asked, 'Which mountain is that?'

On hearing Tamemasa say, 'That's the famous Mount Stallion,'
Shigeyuki said:

Yuki fureba ashige ni miyuru Ikoma yama   [5–7–5]
Because it snows Mount Stallion looks piebald

"Tamemasa made several attempts to cap it, but however he
tried, he could not. Seeing this, a lowly samurai in Tamemasa's
bodyguard did. It happened like this. When Tamemasa seemed
not to be succeeding, the man loudly coughed for attention and
came forward out of his peers on his knees. His intention was
so obvious that Shigeyuki said, 'Kōbunta appears to be able
to cap it.' But Tamemasa said, 'It's ludicrous. This man's so
rude,' pushed him back, and did not allow him to say what he
wanted to. So Kōbunta withdrew to his seat, and that was that.
Still, Tamemasa couldn't come up with a cap, and a while
passed. So, disappointed, he said, 'Well, in that case, spit it
out. How did you cap it?' Kōbunta for some time looked re-
sentful and would not say anything, but at Shigeyuki's repeated
urgings, he finally did:

itsu natsukage ni naramu to suramu   [7–7]
when will summer bring chestnuts?

"Tamemasa clucked his tongue, taken aback. But Shigeyuki,
hearing it, stood up and danced. He was so overwhelmed he
took off his clothes and gave them to Kōbunta as a reward.
Truly, the way he gave his clothes and walked away in dignity
was, I'm told, quite marvelous."

The other anecdote comes eight hundred years later, from
Fukui Kyūzō (1867–1951), one of the first modern scholars to
look into renga systematically. Most of the tales and poems his
mother told him and recited for him when he was a child merely
cast "vague shadows on the canvas of my mind," he says, but
there is "one image that, though faint, still remains unerased":

"I was brought up in the countryside in San'in. Barely twenty-five miles to the east flows the Tade River where Minamoto no Raikō [died 1021, a military leader] is said to have composed renga with his wife, Sagami, in a boat. . . . My mother's story, as I remember, took place [farther east] on the road to Tango. An old and withered pilgrim in a black robe and wearing a sedge hat was trudging along the northern coast. The time was early summer, green leaves on the further coast looked almost wet in their freshness. When he reached a fork on the road, he stopped plying his stick, took down from his back his travel casket, its lacquer peeled off somewhat, and was resting, bathed in the clear wind. A chickadee flew by and perched near the casket; soon it began looking for a chance to get in it. A bright-looking young man who happened by was quick to notice it; he gave it a moment's thought, then looked quite pleased with himself. He said to himself, 'Isn't this fun!' and loudly to the pilgrim:

Shijūkara wa oi no naka ni zo iri ni keri   [6–7–5]
A chickadee has gone into the travel casket

"Repeating the phrase, the youth urged the pilgrim to cap it with a second half. The pilgrim turned a nonplussed look to the young man and said he was only a pilgrim visiting from province to province, with no learning at all, that he knew nothing about poetry or scholarship. He asked if he could reach his home town, Obama, faster by taking the left road at that point; he couldn't decide because he didn't know which was the shorter way. He begged the youth to tell him. But the youth, obviously a lover of renga, still kept repeating the first half and insisted that the pilgrim come up with something. The pilgrim, unconcerned about the request, just said:

Wakasa ni kaeru michi ga shiritai   [7–7]
I'd like to know the road to Wakasa

"At this, the young man clapped his hands and delightedly exclaimed, 'That's it! That's it! Now we have a wonderful renga!' Then he told the pilgrim the road to take and walked away."

Each story reveals three elements of renga and its composition: form based on the syllabic patterns of 5–7–5 and 7–7; joining of verse entities to make a larger whole; and verse writing that involves more than one person.

As for form, the two examples of renga here are both *tan-renga* (short renga), in the minimum combination of two parts, and those two parts are what make up the 5-7-5-7-7–syllable tanka form; in each case, the initial observation is made in 5-7-5 syllables (one is hypermetric), followed by a response in 7-7 syllables. Even though quite early in the development of renga two-part pieces in the reversed pattern of 7-7-5-7-5 syllables began to be composed, it is significant that the first recorded renga was in fact a tanka. An unidentifed nun who meant to turn out a straightforward tanka became lost after composing the 5-8-5–syllable (hypermetric) "head part":

Saho gawa no mizu o sekiagete ueshi ta o
We dammed the water of Saho River and planted the paddies

which Ōtomo no Yakamochi (716–85?) completed by providing an 8-7–syllable (hypermetric) "end part:"

kareru hatsu-ii wa hitori naru beshi
but I'll harvest and eat the first rice by myself

This collaboration appears as poem number 1635 in the *Man'-yōshū* (Collection of Ten Thousand Leaves), compiled in the second half of the eighth century, and is the only one of its kind in that vast anthology containing more than forty-five hundred poems. The primacy of tanka as the prototype of renga continued in the longer combinations that were attempted later: all of them consisted of even numbers of parts when, as in *chōka* (long song), an extra part could have been added at the end of a sequence.

As to the joining of verse units, in each of the two examples cited the two parts are more or less separate, and they are "linked" primarily by form (to make a tanka). In content, what links the parts together in the exchange between Shigeyuki and Kōbunta is wordplay: *ashige* means both "piebald" and "terrible," and *natsukage,* "brown with dark spots" and "summer foliage." (My translation brings out only half of the original effect.) In the other exchange, it is association: the reader, like the young man, presumes that the sight of a chickadee going into a travel casket fuels the desire to go home. The relative independence of each part is vital because in linked poetry the sense of linking must be maintained and that is greatly enhanced by the element of unexpectedness in transition.

Concerning the involvement of at least two persons, in the episodes above, Kōbunta is considered too lowly for the occasion by the governor Tamemasa, and the pilgrim's response is accidental, but neither Shigeyuki nor the young man intends to supply the "link" himself. Though composing renga alone was fashionable in some periods later in the development of the form, the assumption of two or more participants in the writing of a single poem is the basis of renga in concept and execution. And since any such group effort requires a meeting of the participants, the place and the occasion are far more important in renga than in most other forms of poetry. Partly for that reason, some have said that reading a renga text is like reading a play.

How did renga come into being? There are, I think, three factors that contributed to its birth and sustained its development. One is the tendency of tanka—the major poetic form before renga—to break up into two parts, the first half (5-7-5 syllables) and the second (7-7 syllables). Possibly under the influence of Chinese poetry employing five- and seven-character lines, Japanese poets established five- and seven- syllable units as the basis of versification by the seventh century. As we can see in the *Kojiki* (Record of Ancient Matters), compiled in 712, and the *Man'yōshū,* there were in the beginning several poetic forms, of which tanka and chōka were prominent. A chōka consists of three or more five- and seven-syllable patterns, usually ending with an extra seven-syllable part. Curiously, tanka was the form used for the envoy or envoys to a chōka, when *kata-uta* (half song) of 5-7-7 syllables might have been a more logical choice. At any rate, because of the early tendency for the five- and seven-syllable combination to achieve some basic coherence in meaning, and perhaps because of the repetition of the same combination in chōka, early tanka more often than not have a pause after the first 5-7 syllables, as in the one that the empress Yamato wrote for her husband, Tenji, in 671, when he was ill (*Man'yōshū*, no. 147):

Ama no hara furisake mireba   [5–7]
ōkimi no mi-inochi wa nagaku ama tarashitari   [5–8–7]

When I turn to look at the Plain of Heaven,
Your Majesty's life is long, enough to fill out Heaven

But gradually a majority of tanka began to be written with a pause after the 5-7-5 syllables. One of the more famous pieces by Ōtomo no Yakamochi, written in 753, is a good example (*Man'yōshū*, no. 4292):

Uraura ni tereru haru-hi ni hibari agari   [5–7–6]
kokoro ganashi mo hitori shi omoeba   [7–8]

On this languidly shining spring day, skylarks rise;
I am saddened at heart, thinking alone

This 5-7-5–break–7-7 pattern increased in importance in the ensuing centuries until, by the year 1200, it became a technique that characterized the tanka poetry of the period. And the technique, when combined with an attempt to present two images or ideas of considerable independence in a single tanka, produced many pieces that distinctly resemble renga. The following piece (*Shin Kokinshū* [New Collection of Ancient and Modern Poems], no. 36) by the retired emperor Gotoba (1180–

1239), is not only considered illustrative of the development, but it is also alluded to in the opening part of the most famous one-hundred-part renga, *Three Poets at Minase,* of which we will see excerpts later:

Miwataseba yamamoto kasumu Minase-gawa   [5–7–5]
yūbe wa aki to nani omoiken   [7–7]

As I look out, the hill-base is hazy along Minase River—why did I think the evening was for autumn alone?

In the first part Gotoba gives a simple description of a landscape, although there are a few things here that were obvious to his contemporaries, but are not to us: "hazy" indicates spring; the word is appreciative, not depreciatory; and Minase was also a place where Gotoba had a palace built. In the second part the poet makes a subjective, abstract, even puzzling statement— a twist on the literary notion harking back to an observation made by Sei Shōnagon (active around 1000) that in autumn the best time of the day is the evening (*Pillow Book,* chapter 1). The two parts could have been written independently, or by different poets.

A second factor that provided a basis for renga is the Japanese poets' strong inclination to make verse composition a group activity. More than 40 of the 112 poems in the *Kojiki* are exchanges between demigods, princes and princesses, and other characters. The *Man'yōshū,* in addition to many similar exchanges and poems composed at various gatherings, has groups of questions and replies in tanka form. Tanka are basically used to be exchanged in the ninth century *Tales of Ise,* a collection of episodes in which Ariwara no Narihira (825–80) plays the role of Don Juan. Toward the end of the same century, more formal *uta-awase* (tanka matches) began to be held, and even though the idea was a simple one of subjecting tanka to judgment in pairs, detailed rules and procedures were established for them before long. Some official tanka matches were evidently as elaborate and festal as other court contests, such as archery, wrestling, and horse-racing, with sumptuous prizes readied for the winners. Some others, especially in a later period, were of a more serious nature where poetic theories were tested, diction refined, and ideas explored. From both kinds, renga gained a good deal: from the festal kind, it strengthened the sense of fun and competitiveness; from the serious kind, it inherited concepts such as *yūgen,* which may be translated "subdued elegance," and ideas such as the one of making one hundred parts the standard unit of composition. Most important was the favorable attitude the poets took to writing poetry as and for a group.

In this, Nijō Yoshimoto (1320–88), who brought out the first important anthology of renga, was right in tracing the origin of the form to two-person utterances that have little to do with the form as we know it. Pointing to the assertion of Urabe Kanetaka, a Shintoist in the thirteenth century, Yoshimoto indicates he named his anthology, completed in 1356, *Tsukuba-shū* (Tsukuba Collection), because of the following passage in the *Nihon Shoki* (History of Japan), compiled in 720:

"Having already pacified Ezo, [Prince Yamato Takeru] returned from the province of Hitakami, passed through Hitachi to the southwest, and reached the province of Kai where he rested at the palace of Sakaori. Then he had torches lit and had his meal. That night in a song he asked his attendants:

Niibari Tsukuba o sugite iku yo ka netsuru   [4–7–7]
Since passing Niibari and Tsukuba, how many nights have we slept?

"The many attendants were unable to reply. But there happened to be a man lighting the torches. Following the prince's song with a second half, he said with a song:

Kaga nabete yo ni wa kokono yo hi ni wa tō ka o   [5–7–7]
Add up the days, and of nights there are nine nights, of days, ten days.

"Thereupon, the prince praised the torch-tender for his talent and rewarded him amply."

The "songs" here are 5-7-7–syllable katauta (the first one hypometric), called "half songs" because two of them are needed to make a complete sedōka (repeat song). In *Tsukuba Mondō* (Questions and Answers on Tsukuba), a treatise on renga he wrote after completing the anthology, Yoshimoto pushed the date of the origin further back to the first words exchanged between Izanagi and Izanami, the first male and female deities in Japanese mythology. In ascribing such antiquity to renga, he was no doubt attempting to increase the prestige of the form; but he also must have felt that was justified because, in his view, a renga was "a song uttered by two persons."

There is a third factor: likely Chinese influence. China had its counterpart of renga, known as *lien-chü,* with its first known example dating from the Chin Dynasty (265–420); also, Po Chü-yi (772–846), who was popular among Japanese poets to the point of deification, left eleven lien-chü he wrote with his friends. Although by the time Yoshimoto mentioned lien-chü in relation to renga, renga had developed into an art far more complex than anything contemplated for lien-chü, it is safe to assume that lien-chü gave renga at least a nudge in its formative period.

Minamoto no Toshiyori, who wrote the piebald/chestnuts episode, was the first to accord a prominent status to renga. And it was about time. In his treatise, *Zuinō,* he observed, "It is renga that appears as popular in this degraded world as in the past," suggesting that not many examples from the past remained because people neglected to "put them on paper." Even so, he manages to cite about forty renga, some with stories like the one on the snowy morning—the episode which, if the attribution is credible, describes an incident toward the end of the tenth century. Indeed, poets began to compose renga rather regularly during the same century, and collections from that and the next century contain smatterings of renga. But it was Toshiyori who gave the form more than accidental attention. In addition to the inclusion of a large number of renga, the *Zuinō* is notable for the first technical observation made on the form: whether to begin a two-part renga with 5-7-5– or 7-7–syllable lines is "up to you," he says, but either way, you must "finish saying in your part what you have to say," for it is no good to oblige whoever follows you to feel forced. In the *Kin'yōshū* (Collection of Gold-leafed Poems), the imperial anthology of which he was the sole editor, Toshiyori not only selected nineteen two-part renga but also honored them with a separate category. About the same time he completed the anthology—a few years before his death —he collected his own poems in *Samboku Kikashū* (Collection of a Do-Nothing's Eccentric Poems), and included in it fifty-nine renga. Later commentators distinguished Toshiyori for his preference for what was contemporary over what was approved by tradition, partly because of his stress on renga.

If Toshiyori was the first to recognize the importance of linked poetry, the retired emperor Gotoba was the first to give the form the imperial stamp as something to be enjoyed officially. Gotoba is called "retired emperor," because he gave up the throne at the age of eighteen, in 1198, abdication at a young age being routine at the time. But he was not at all retiring; his fame rests mostly on what he did after retirement. He fully lived his age, the period when the power of the aristocracy finally declined and was replaced by the power of the military. He was made emperor at age four because the emperor Antoku (1178–85) was practically abducted by the then ruling military clan, the Taira, as they fled another clan, the Minamoto. In 1221 Gotoba raised an army against the military government established by the Minamoto; his forces were trounced in a month, and he was exiled to the remote island of Oki where he died. Gotoba's was also a period when court poetry, under his driving force, flourished for the last time. On his orders the *Wakadokoro* (Poetry Office) was revived in the seventh month of 1201, and the compilation of the eighth anthology of Japanese poetry, *Shin Kokinshū,* began four months later. His chroniclers tell us that the retired emperor excelled both in military and literary ways, but we now remember him as a literary commander in chief. His military adventure was quashed as soon as it began, but the *Shin Kokinshū,* on which he worked hard as its real editor, has survived as a great anthology despite the ups and downs of its reputation since then.

A quick study in most things, Gotoba was also imperious. For renga gatherings, he would suddenly summon his courtiers at any time of the day, no matter what the weather. Fujiwara no Teika (1162–1241), from whose *Meigetsuki* (Diary of the Bright Moon) we learn many such things in great detail, reports that during the twelfth month of 1212 he had to dash to the palace at least twice—on one occasion, through the furious rain, and on another, just when he was about to go to bed. On the latter occasion, not a nameless messenger but Minamoto no Ienaga (died 1234?), the deputy chief of the Poetry Office, came as Gotoba's delegate, and Teika "galloped to the palace in consternation." When people were gathered, Gotoba's preferred method was to divide them into *ushin* ("mind-possessing," or professional) and *mushin* ("mind-lacking," or nonprofessional) groups and let them compete. According to Teika, the method came about because nonprofessional poets once banded together and tried to beat professional poets with "mad renga," or renga using non-poetic diction—a challenge that the professional poets accepted on their own terms, using "regular," or poetic, diction; when Gotoba heard about this, he adopted the grouping. During one such competition, held on the eleventh of the eighth month of 1206, Gotoba decreed that the group that first came up with six consecutive parts would be the winner. As soon as one side, which happened to be his, did, he ordered the opposing group out of the room into the garden where they were made to "sit directly," presumably on the pebbles, "with their foreheads lowered to the ground." "The weather was spectacular," Teika adds. He was on Gotoba's side, of course.

Such impetuosity and delight in wielding imperial power notwithstanding, Gotoba wouldn't have been Gotoba had he not been generous with prizes. At first, paper, a valuable commodity at the time, was the main prize, but gradually prizes became extravagant. For example, at a gathering on the fourteenth of the fourth month, 1217, which covered renga as well as other forms of poetry, such a great quantity of brocaded silk fabric imported from China was put up as prizes that some winners presented unseemly sights at the end of the gathering, unable to leave the room graciously with the heaps of fabric they had won.

What kind of renga did Gotoba and his servants compose? As far as we can tell from Teika's diary, the length ranged from thirty to more than one hundred parts. Of the various lengths, the set of one hundred was the most frequently used, probably because by then the unit of that number was standard in formal tanka composition. However, the length was not something established, but was still subject to the exigencies of the occasion. At the gathering toward the end of the year 1212—for which Teika had to abandon his hope of having a good night's sleep after a full day and rush to the palace on horseback—the word from the retired emperor was that the parts "be limited to thirty because it was very late at night." At the 1217 gathering where the winners' manner of disposing of their prizes embarrassed Teika, the links were limited to fifty, probably because of the other contests to be taken care of.

The linking technique was primarily based on *fushimono*, incorporating in each part something belonging to a category of references or a set of items that suggest certain things. Such categories and sets Teika cites in his diary are: five colors; things that float or sink; birds and fish; black and white; trees and personal names (twenty-fifth of the twelfth month, 1212: Teika notes that the rule specifying the use of the personal names of contemporaries resulted in inclusion of the name of a minister and asks prissily, "Though this is just a game, should such a thing be tolerated?"); personal names and plants; fish and names of rivers; provinces and the names of the chapters of *The Tale of Genji*; and plants and trees. There is one more combination, the first part of which I do not understand, even though Teika gives an example. Its second part, *sanji chūryaku*, is clear, however; you choose a word consisting of three characters that will still make sense after the elimination of the middle character; in Teika's example, *a-ka-ki* (red) makes sense as *a-ki* (autumn)—an English example is *aim*, which makes sense as *am*. The participants on that day (twenty-eighth of the eighth month, 1214) were expected to incorporate the first fushimono in 5-7-5–syllable parts, and the second, in 7-7–syllable parts. Teika says that "both parts were difficult to accomplish"—so much so that, leaving the gathering, the participants "looked disgusted. But that was true of everyone, the higher lords down. So why should I alone be sober about it?"

To give an example of renga using the fushimono technique, here is a two-part set incorporating something white and something black. Someone said in 7-7 syllables:

> *wata no kuzu nite hitai o zo yū*
> that forehead pad is made of used cotton

Hitai-wata (here separated and used in different parts of speech) is a wad of raw cotton used by old women to keep their heads warm, so the description suggests an old woman. In response, Teika came up with a link of 5-7-5 syllables (*Tsukubashū*, no. 1987):

ō-hige no o-kurumazoi no kita-omote
a massively bearded ox-cart attendant, a north-front guard

"North-front" refers to the north side of the imperial palace where a squad of warriors was stationed. Linked to this, the "forehead pad" becomes part of the headgear worn by an imperial guard, who looks rather intimidating but is dressed somewhat shabbily. In this combination, "cotton" suggests white, and "beard," black. In another example touching on the same set of colors, someone said in 5-7-5 syllables:

otomego ga Katsuragi yama o haru kakete
a hint of spring like a maiden, over Mount Wig

Here, "wig" is thought to suggest black. To this, Fujiwara no Ietaka (1158–1237) responded in 7-7 syllables (*Tsukubashū*, no. 11):

  kasume do imada mine no shira-yuki
  though it's hazy, white snow remains on its peak

Haze or haziness is, by literary convention, considered a manifestation of spring.

These two sets of two-part renga were possibly in the same group of a hundred parts. But how more than two parts were linked by any other technique than fushimono is not entirely clear for the simple reason that no complete groups remain from Gotoba's gatherings. Were such groups of varying lengths —for example, composed of clusters of two-part renga more or less independent of each other? Or were they like later renga in which any two consecutive parts are linked but three are not? Probably many, if not all, were composed in the latter fashion; the techniques of association and progression were highly polished by Gotoba himself in arranging tanka, and several sets of three and four consecutive parts from his time included in the *Tsukubashū* show the linking of AB, BC, and so forth. Here is a set of three, the last two of which were by the retired emperor (*Tsukubashū*, nos. 1302, 1755):

  Mimuro no yama wa iro masarikeri
  Mount Mimuro has intensified its color

  kure kakaru mine ni hikage no sasu mama ni
  darkness falling, the peak remains in the shining sun

    konata no sato o isogu tabibito
    in a village this side a traveler hurries

Mount Mimuro is noted for its maple trees, so the anonymous first part belongs to the "autumn" category. (Following the court tanka tradition, every renga part was expected to fall into one of the categories such as spring, summer, autumn, winter,

Shintoism, Buddhism, love, miscellaneous, traveling, and felicitations.) Writing the second, Gotoba switches the category to non-specific "miscellaneous." He then comes up with his own link, changing the category to that of "traveling"; in doing so, he throws in a human figure, a definable one at that (the person "hurries"), to create the foreground against the background of a distant mountain. The sequence is in a mode typical of the renga as we know it: the focus and sentiment keep changing to make a series of "shifting pairs of tableaux." It is a brilliant execution.

This attribution of two consecutive parts to Gotoba and that of five to Teika—numbers 1785, 492, 770, 268, and 1007— suggest a possibility of solo renga composition. But they are likely to be the results of the competitive writing where anyone who could come up with the next acceptable link was to add to his glory. Whatever the linking technique, one thing is certain: Gotoba greatly helped make the unit of one hundred parts a standard length, so that his third son, the emperor Juntoku (1197–1242), could treat it as the norm in his treatise on poetry, *Yakumo Mishō* (Some Thoughts on Yakumo).

The next important figure came a century later: Nijō Yoshimoto, the compiler of the *Tsukubashū* anthology. Through his prestige as the highest ranking official at the court, he succeeded in acquiring the "semi-imperial" status for the anthology, thereby exalting the position of renga to close to that of formal tanka. He made other important contributions. He wrote several essays in an attempt to define an attitude toward renga and its composition; he also established a set of rules—"for my circle," he said characteristically, but "not for the future" —by sifting through the existing rules, devising new ones where necessary. In all this, Yoshimoto was helped and guided by the premier renga poet of the time, Monk Gusai (1282–1376), although Gusai, a non-court poet, had to remain in the background.

The renga rules, as written down by Yoshimoto and revised by later poets, including Bashō, may be grouped into three kinds: general, specific, and optional.

• General Rules •

FORM Alternating 5-7-5– and 7-7–syllable parts; begin with a 5-7-5–syllable part and end with a 7-7–syllable part. Any two consecutive parts must make an intelligible, independent whole, but three may not: AB, BC, CD, but not ABC, BCDE, DEF, and so on.

LENGTH One hundred parts, or an equivalent of fifty tanka, was standard before Bashō's time; thereafter, thirty-six parts. Sequences of seven hundred, one thousand, and ten thousand parts are all multiplications of the standard arrangement of one hundred parts. There are also sequences of forty-four, fifty, and so forth; in theory, any length is admissible.

LINKING The essence and backbone of renga. Renga linking presupposes what follows will be by a different hand, and that makes vital, even inevitable, the element of surprise, however mundane, tenuous, illogical, or far-fetched. Although renga following the court tradition became enmeshed in rules and restrictions, the element of surprise, the possibility that one can show one's wit among one's peers, remained and, let us hope, remains the attraction of the renga form. The form also presupposes that an infinite variety of reactions is possible to a given description or statement. As Yoshimoto said, "The linking is up to the writer's attitude, and there shouldn't be anything set about this." He felt most of the linking techniques might be categorized as follows:

Hirazuke (straight linking): linking based upon such word pairs as birds—trees, bees—honey, boy—girl, and so on. An example:

tsuki ni mo miba ya ochi no yama no ha   [7–7]
I'd like to see those distant rims of mountains under the moon

shigururu o iro naru mine no yomo no sora   [5–7–5]
though in shower the peaks all around are colorful against the
  sky

Yotsude (two for two): a combination of two items provoking
a combination of two items, as in East/West—moon/sun.

hidari mo migi mo saoshika no koe   [7–7]
left and right, stags call

kariudo no yumi tori ya tori iru yama ni   [5–7–5]
as the hunter climbs the mountain with a bow, with arrows

In the original, "left and right" are supposed to be corresponsive
to "with a bow, with arrows," or at least double-enumerative.
  Keiki (landscape): a description of a landscape followed by
another, without any ostentatious verbal display. The stress is
on naturalness, and the technique is considered most important
in court or orthodox renga. An example:

ashibe ni shiroki sagi no hito-tsure   [7–7]
white along the reed edge, a pair of herons

ame ochiru irie no nami ni yama kurete   [5–7–5]
as the rain falls into the inlet waves, the mountain grows dark

Kokoro-zuke (linking "by heart"): linking by association.

muma wa are domo kachi nite zo yuku   [7–7]
I have a horse but I am going on foot

asaborake yo no ma ni tsumoru yuki o mite   [5–7–5]
having seen at daybreak the snow that piled up during the night

A good many interpretations of the relation between the snow
and not using the horse may be possible, but the relation is cer-
tainly not mechanical. The person who wrote about the snow
tried to echo a sentiment perceived in the foregoing observa-
tion.

Kotoba-zuke (linking by word): verbal association and punning are the major means. Verbal association here is of a restrictive kind; as a result of the tendency in the rarefied world of Japanese court poetry to require "precedents" for words, phrases, and ideas, certain words and phrases were associated only with certain others, as in "pine tree" associated with "wisteria." Some are easy to see, such as "splash" prompting the image of "waves," but even then certain images are supposed to be connected only to certain others. Linking by verbal association of this kind is done by gathering as many associated words, phrases, and images as possible. Punning is easier—though only to explain; for the translator, it is a bane. A pun in Japanese can be as complex as one in English, with possibly one important difference: in Japanese court poetry and in "serious" renga influenced by it, a pun does not necessarily add a knowing, leery tone. An example:

uramite mo nao nagusami ni keri	[7–7]
matsubara no shiohi ni kakaru tabi no michi	[5–7–5]

The 7-7 syllables may be translated, "I am resentful but feel consoled," at one level. But *uramite* (resentful) can also be *ura mite* (looking at the bay or the reverse side), and it is one of the meanings the latter suggests that the person who wrote the 5-7-5 syllables took: "Looking at the bay I still feel consoled." His link may be translated: "the road I take, traveling, leads into the tideland near a grove of pines." *Ura* (bay, cove) and *matsubara* (pine grove) are traditionally associated with each other.

Uzumi-ku (buried allusion): in Yoshimoto's words, linking which "on the surface does not seem achieved," but which "underneath has a profound sentiment" that justifies it. The technique is one of allusion that is not obvious but merely suggested, as in:

naki yowaritaru higurashi no koe	[7–7]
clear-tone cicadas' voices, now enfeebled	

uki aki ni tare yamazato o tazunuran [5–7–5]
in this depressing autumn who'd visit this mountain village?

In pointing to the "Yadorigi" chapter of *The Tale of Genji* as the source of the allusion "buried" in this pair, a commentator notes that only two words, *higurashi* (clear-toned cicadas) and *yamazato* (mountain village), are actually traceable to the alleged original episode.

Yosei (overtone): a suggestive description. An example:

tōki kinuta no koe kikoyu nari [7–7]
I hear the sound of a distant mallet

tsuki no yo no fuke yuku mama ni shizumarite [5–7–5]
the moonlit night grows late, the air quiet

The mallet is one used for fulling cloth, and because of poems by Po Chü-yi and other Chinese poets, the utensil is thought of as being used at night and its sound is expected to provoke an acute sense of solitude. In this pair, the link, by describing a quiet moonlit night, suggests a woman fulling cloth and thinking of her husband sent far away as a soldier or for some other reason not home.

Sōtai (contrast): in Yoshimoto's words, "as in spring/autumn, morning/evening, mountain/field." An example (*Tsukubashū*, no. 137):

towareneba nochi no ashita mo iza shirazu [5–7–5]
no one visits me, and I know of no "morning after"

kyō miru hana no yuki no yūgure [7–7]
the flowers seen today will be snow in the evening

Hikichigae (contrariness): like some other techniques, this is possible because of stock responses established and expected in court poetry. Cherry blossoms past their prime, for example, scatter like snow at the slightest provocation; so a court poet, in composing a piece on this plant, was expected to say he did not want the wind to blow. Hikichigae is a technique of going against that sentiment. Consider the following linking:

matsu o tonari no yamazato no haru [7–7]
  a pine tree adjacent in this mountain village, it's spring

chiru o miru yoso no hana ni wa kaze machite [5–7–5]
seeing cherries scatter I wait for the wind—the tree's someone
  else's

The pine tree is an evergreen, an object that suggests eternity
and therefore felicitousness. The poet of the first part is thus
congratulating himself for the good fortune of having gone
through the winter with a pine tree, which stands either in his
neighbor's garden or, if it's in his, next to something else,
possibly a cherry tree. Picking this up, the next poet notes that
not only the pine tree but also the cherry tree is his neighbor's
and hopes the wind will blow so that he may enjoy the scattering
of the flowers. (The second remark contains, in addition to
contrariness to an accepted attitude, a seemingly mean wish
that a wind will blow because the cherry tree is someone else's.
The wish is not exactly an expression of meanness, however.
It is rather an expression of the state of mind variously described
as *fūga, fūryū,* or *fūkyō*—unworldliness, quaintness, eccentricity,
"poetic dementia." This particular brand of conceit, along
with contrariness, will play an increasingly important role in
renga.)

  Kakushi-dai (hidden topic): essentially, puns (see kotoba-zuke).
Puns in this category, often encompassing two or more words,
tend to be independent of the surface meaning of a given state-
ment (as in fishing out from the immediately preceding part of
this sentence things like "dent of the surface" and "mean-
spirited ace surfer"). An example (*Tsukubashū,* no. 1046):

tsuki no wazuka ni kasumu yūgure [7–7]
  the moon is slightly hazy this evening

kuma no sumu utsuhogi nagara hana sakite [5–7–5]
though a hollow tree where a bear lives, it puts on blossoms

The introduction of *kuma* (bear) is possible because *tsuki-no-wa* (lunar ring) can refer to one of the two species of bear known in Japan, *tsukinowa-guma,* so-called for the white crescent patch it has under its neck. It may be seen, however, that unlike the resentful/bay/reverse-side pun in the example cited in the kotoba-zuke section, *tsuki-no-wa* is somewhat forced and without it the rest of the sentence does not make sense.

Honka (allusion to a tanka): imitative of a technique in court tanka writing. The degree and manner of allusion in tanka may be known from Teika's observation in *Eiga Taigai* (Outline for Composing Tanka), written in 1222: "To borrow as many as three units out of the five is quite excessive and results in a lack of novelty; to borrow two units plus three or four syllables is admissible." In other words, you may duplicate half or more of someone else's composition in your own. There are some injunctions for allusion in renga. One of them is that you may not allude to the same tanka in three consecutive parts. Another is that you may not allude to poets who wrote after the compilation of the *Shin Kokinshū* in 1205.

Honzetsu (allusion to a well-known story, anecdote, or Chinese poem): a technique similar to honka. The difference between this and uzumi-ku is that honzetsu is overt, uzumi-ku covert.

Nadokoro (famous places): incorporation of the names of famous places. The technique is the same as kakushi-dai, except that the category of words to be used is limited to place names. In Yoshimoto's examples, *kono yama no onore* (I, on this mountain) "hides" the name of a mountain, Ono, and *shitakusa no oi so no mori* (the forest where low grass grows), the name of a village, Oiso. Yoshimoto cautions against the frequent use of this technique, probably because place names tend to make the parts incorporating them too conspicuous.

Some later poets added to the description of linking techniques and some, like Bashō, devised new terms. But as Yoshimoto said, "Ordinarily, linking should be made through association 'by heart' or 'by word.' " In fact, all modes of linking may be said to be based on association. The importance of linking can hardly be overstated. Renga anthologies, such as the *Tsukubashū*, often consist of two-part excerpts from longer sequences, rather than sequences themselves. Also, *maeku-zuke* or *tsukeai*, links in the minimum combination of two parts, were often composed independent of sequences.

The following is a selection of links by Yoshimoto and Monk Gusai, from the *Tsukubashū*: the number at the end of each pair is that in the anthology. As elsewhere in this book, the 7-7–syllable parts are indented, while the 5-7-5–syllable parts are not.

By Yoshimoto

on the mountain stags call, in the field insects chirp

at each object I'm saddened in the autumn evening   (299)

~

a screech—that must be a mountain flying squirrel

at daybreak the moon has dropped behind a stand of trees   (384)

~

just a hint, but this rubbed-on fragrance

my sleeve, which I used for someone's pillow   (829)

~

I don't know how you'll change after you do

just this one night, for a memory, for a dream   (838)

~

against my own thoughts I set out on a journey

before dawn, confused by the moon, a rooster calls   (1225)

~

the distant mountain appears to swallow the moon

large Koshi boat for capturing whales, beware!   (1902)

By Monk Gusai

asking for an inn at a place I didn't dream of

led by the cherry blossoms I must have forgotten myself　　(97)

~

come to think of it, this must be the last moment

to the cherry blossoms scattering in the evening rain, a gust
down the hill　　(156)

~

fallen leaves surely, lying on the water

they're the nesting birds unable to leave the summer river inlet
(247)

~

the old mansion is not aware of the fall

an ownerless boat abandoned on the bay carries the moon
(389)

~

retributions for my crime—come what may

the moon remains above the hunting ground as dawn breaks
(561)

~

the moon is so cold I wish I had a friend to visit me

the field temple bell is distant this autumn night　　(631)

~

to my dreaming pillow comes the faint moonlight

as I trace how we made love before you died　　(764)

~

for climbing up the mountain there's only one trail

his hut can't be seen but smoke rises through the valley trees
(1243)

~

responding to the wind, the sound of bay waves

in the village across the river lives a friend of mine   (1366)

~

the feeling of spring is in the evening bell

all my expectations gone now—I'm that old   (1504)

~

now it's past, I forget what happened yesterday

travelers change at the inn, it's evening   (1758)

~

they laugh but aren't belittling him

the flock of crows at the forest treetops, a hawk above   (1931)

DEVELOPMENT   A hundred-part sequence was written on four sheets of paper, each folded once and holes made at one end to tie the four folded sheets together. One of the two outsides of each folded sheet was called the "front," and the other, the "back." The front of the first sheet had the first eight parts of the sequence; the back of the first sheet, the fronts and backs of the second and third sheets, and the front of the fourth sheet, each had fourteen parts; and the back of the fourth sheet, eight, making a total of one hundred parts. Nothing was written on the insides of the four folded sheets.

The sequential development of a renga so arranged is explained by using the musical terminology *jo-ha-kyū* (in one translation, introduction, elaboration, and finale; in another, preface, development, and fast finale). According to Yoshimoto, "Through the front of the first sheet, you should do graceful renga. Even with particles you shouldn't do anything of levity. Beginning with the second sheet, you should make exciting phrases, and make the third and fourth sheets particularly attractive. . . . The first sheet should be the *jo*, the second sheet *ha*, and the third and fourth sheets *kyū*." As Yoshimoto stressed, rules change. By the time of Tani Sōboku (1488?–

1545), the *jo* covered the section through the front of the
second sheet or the first thirty-six parts, *ha* through the end of
the third sheet or the next forty-two parts, and *kyū* the re-
mainder or the last twenty-two parts. Later, the sections for
the three designations changed further, so that the first eight
parts became *jo,* the following eighty-four parts *ha,* and the
last eight parts *kyū*.

During Bashō's time, the preferred length also changed,
from one hundred to thirty-six parts, and the shorter sequence
was set down on two sheets of paper, similarly folded, with its
parts distributed 6, 12, 12, 6. Bashō appears not to have left
definitive words on sequential development; he was content
merely to say, "A sequence uniform from beginning to end
would be ugly to look at." But his sense of it was evidently
strong enough to prompt Mukai Kyorai (1651–1704), one of
his disciples, to say: "In a sequence, you should compose the
front uneventfully. From the back of the first sheet to the
middle of the front of the second sheet, there should be ec-
centric turns and twists. From there into the back of the
second sheet, you should purl along, composing unpainstakingly.
As you approach the end, people begin to tire of one another,
so that if you still try to turn out good pieces, you tend to end
up, on the contrary, with difficult, unsuccessful ones. However,
this does not mean that a renga gathering must be blocked
from turning out good pieces when it is bouncing along to the
very last piece. It means you should not strive for good pieces."
Kyorai's observation hints at the possibility that he had in mind
four, rather than three, stages of development for a sequence.
But the important point is to lay some pattern; otherwise, a
renga sequence may tend to disperse.

QUALITY OF EACH PART Implicit in Kyorai's words is the
idea that one need not be consis-
tently good in renga. Yoshimoto was explicit about it, saying
that a renga sequence ought to consist of impressive and not-so-
impressive pieces, and that a good poet should not contribute

more than two or three impressive pieces in one session. The words he used for impressive and not-so-impressive are textile terms, *umon* (prints or design) and *mumon* (solids or ground). The practice of deliberately blending umon and mumon pieces in a sequence appears to go back to the time of the retired emperor Gotoba and before, when a hundred tanka were composed as a unit; for such a sequence not more than ten impressive pieces at the most were written, and they were placed throughout the sequence in such a way as to make them stand out among routine pieces. The practice derives in part from aesthetic consider-ations; for example, a sequence of one hundred tanka, each a shining example of poetry, may have the danger of looking like, as a friend of mine put it, "a series of firecrackers." But it is also based on a realistic assessment of the situation; for, as Yoshimoto said, "How is it possible to show excellence in every piece?" To excel in every piece and at every turn may not be always impossible, but an attempt to do so would put an undue strain on the poet. It is good to remember that Iio Sōgi (1421–1502), considered the paragon of renga writers, was noted for his ability to be retiring, contributing mumon pieces more often than most.

INTENSITY OF LINKAGE The concept of linkage intensity was developed after Yoshimoto and was particularly stressed by Monk Shinkei (1406–75). Following the observations attributed to Teika, Shinkei said that in renga there ought to be closely connected links and remotely con-nected links, and that outstanding verses were to be found among the latter. In his opinion a remote connection occurred when the linkage was made "by heart," rather than in response to the "style" or "phrasing" of the preceding part. An example he cited as showing a remote linkage:

hajime mo hate mo shiranu yo no naka
in this world one knows neither the beginning nor the end

wada no hara yosete wa kaeru okitsu nami
the waves of the ocean come from offshore and go away

Here the linkage is remote because an abstract observation is
followed by a concrete one. In contrast, in the next pair cited
to show a close linkage, an almost fantastic description is
graphically explained by the link:

kōri no ue ni nami zo tachinuru
waves rise all over the ice

sayuru yo no tsuki no kage no no hana-susuki
clear night: in the moonlit field, flowering pampas grass

DICTION For Yoshimoto, poetic diction was defined by the
court poets; this largely meant the diction found
in *Tales of Ise, The Tale of Genji,* and the first three imperial
anthologies of Japanese poetry: *Kokinshū* (Collection of Ancient
and Modern Poems), *Gosenshū* (Later Collection of Poems),
and *Shūishū* (Collection of Gleaned Poems); for Bashō, it was
daily language.

• Specific Rules •

HOKKU, OPENING PART The 5-7-5–syllable part that opens
a sequence is called the hokku,
and in Yoshimoto's judgment it is "the most important thing."
In a short story (or even in a novel), the opening sentence is
sometimes said to determine the value of what follows. The
idea is the same here. "When the hokku is poorly made,"
Yoshimoto said, "the entire sequence becomes spoiled and
looks bad." It is even possible to divide a sequence into two
groups, the hokku and the rest, and to call the hokku a general,
the remaining parts his soldiers, as Bashō's disciples did.
Naturally, the honor of composing the hokku tended to be

given to the best poet in the group. And because renga was primarily for a group of people gathered to have fun, the opening statement tended to be uplifting and strong. It was also recognized early that the hokku must be more or less self-contained and, as occasional poetry of sorts, incorporate some realistic elements, such as an object quintessential of the time of composition and a phenomenon actually observed at the place of gathering. For these reasons, before long hokku became independent, although independent hokku has been known as haiku only since around 1900 when Masaoka Shiki (1867–1902) gave the term currency.

One outstanding feature of hokku has been to this day the inclusion of *kigo,* seasonal words. The number of kigo was not overwhelming at the outset, with Yoshimoto giving in one list no more than one hundred twenty as especially appropriate for hokku. As might be expected, however, the number quickly increased. A manual of around the year 1800 is said to have listed nearly five thousand. The number has increased further since then, though some poets in this century have advocated rejection of kigo.

The following hokku by Monk Gusai (*Tsukubashū,* no. 2143) is a typical example. It was composed during the Bumpō era (1317–19) at an annual renga meeting at the Kitano Shrine in Kyoto where ten hundred-part sequences were written and dedicated to the shrine deity, Sugawara no Michizane (845–903). Michizane, a scholar-courtier, was regarded as, among other things, the protector and promoter of renga. This hokku topped the first hundred-part sequence:

Sayuru yo wa kaze to tsuki to ni fukenikeri
The lucid night has deepened with wind and with moon

As the wind and the moon were prized for their poetry, Gusai was expressing through this simple description his wish to improve himself as a renga poet. The season of the hokku is assumed to be winter (by the lunar calendar) by its reference to the "lucid night."

30 · FROM RENGA TO HAIKU

WAKIKU OR WAKI,　　Continuing the analogy of the hokku
　　SECOND PART　　with the general of an army, one may
　　　　　　　　　　say the 7-7–syllable second part, called
wakiku or *waki,* is the chief of staff. Supplementing the general's
opening statement on the coming maneuver, the chief of staff
must throw a different light on the same subject but may not
present himself as a dissident. Quoting "a commentator of the
past," Yoshimoto tells us that the wakiku should say "something
different in a manner not detached" from the hokku. In form,
too, this subtle relation holds: the wakiku, in effect, completes
what was originally a tanka, but as part of a renga it must try to
cut away from the preceding part. The custom of having the
guest of honor compose the hokku and the host the wakiku was
well established as early as the time of Yoshimoto and Gusai.

Two other parts of a renga sequence may be mentioned:
daisan, the third part, and *ageku,* the ending part. (All the other
parts are usually called *hiraku,* regular parts.) Though Yoshimoto
seems to have left not many words on the daisan and ageku, by
Bashō's time it was said that their relations to the preceding
parts could be quite tenuous. This is because the chief role of
the third part is to "turn away" or change the subject, and that
of the ending part simply to finish the sequence, almost at any
cost. The sentiment against slowing down toward the end was
strong indeed; it was said that "a good last link does not really
connect" to the preceding one, and the person to write the last
part was even expected to prepare a couple in advance.

MOON AND FLOWER　　As we saw earlier, the hundred-part
　　　　　　　　　　　　sequence was set down on the eight
"outsides" of four folded sheets of paper. In that arrangement
the moon was to be mentioned once on every side (except,
sometimes, the last), and a flower, once on every sheet. In
Yoshimoto's time that was the extent of the requirement. Later,
the exact parts mentioning the moon and flowers were specified,
though even then there was some flexibility. The thirty-six-part
sequence was to have two or three parts describing the moon,

two, a flower. As in the hundred-part sequence, the parts to
mention them were specified, but there seems to have been
much flexibility with Bashō. The moon and flowers—usually
cherry flower—are two prime topics in court poetry, and that
was probably the initial reason for their inclusion in renga. At
the same time, they were used to provide points to return to,
preventing the participants from veering too far off. Also, pre-
paring in advance a couple of candidates for the ageku, or ending
part, was possible, one assumes, because the penultimate part
was to mention a flower. The positions of the moon and flowers
after they were fixed, for a hundred-part sequence, are:

first sheet
front, 8 parts: part 7 to mention the moon
back, 14 parts: part 10, moon; part 13, flower
second sheet
front, 14 parts: part 13, moon
back, 14 parts: part 10, moon; part 13, flower
third sheet
front, 14 parts: part 13, moon
back, 14 parts: part 10, moon; part 13, flower
fourth sheet
front, 14 parts: part 13, moon
back, 8 parts: part 7, flower

And those for a thirty-six-part sequence:

first sheet
front, 6 parts: part 5 to mention the moon
back, 12 parts: part 8, moon; part 11, flower
second sheet
front, 12 parts: part 11, moon
back, 6 parts: part 5, flower

SHIKIMOKU *Shikimoku* may be translated rules or restrictions,
depending on one's emphasis. Either way, shiki-
moku are usually what are meant when "rules" of renga are

spoken of, and they are the most complicated aspect of this poetic form. Some of them are you-mays; most are do-nots. You-mays are intended to give some sense of continuity to the discontinuous form: for example, you may continue to describe spring, autumn, and love in up to five consecutive parts; summer, winter, Shintoism in up to three consecutive parts; and so forth. The do-nots are intended primarily to avoid repetitions and, secondarily, to make certain images stand out. They may be divided into four groups as follows:

(1) Words and images that may not be used in the first ten parts (in the hundred-part sequence). Examples from the "animal" category such as cricket, hawk, duck, sparrow, heron, dove, grebe, fox, monkey, and flying squirrel and those from the "miscellaneous" category such as heavenly maiden, seed sowing, awaking, lonely, and pleased fall into this group. The rationale for banning such words from the opening section is that they are too strong for the introductory section, which ought to be "uneventful."

(2) Words and phrases that may be used only a certain number of times in a sequence. Some that are to be used only once are kerria rose, azalea, warbler, deer, cicada, past, yesterday, morning sun, and woman; twice: pine wind, spring moon, "to miss someone," "to resent someone," and man; three times: cherry, plum, willow, capital (not money, but city), and salt; four times: snow, daybreak, and ice; and several times: moon, haze, mist, tears, wind, smoke, mountain, sky, bay, and garden.

(3) Words and images that may recur only with a certain number of parts in between. For example, if someone has described a house in the seventeenth part, then you cannot talk about "hermitage" at least until the twentieth part. (Placement of at least two parts also applies to certain grammatical endings. For example, if someone has ended his description with the equivalent of a gerund, you must wait for a minimum of two more links to be written before coming up with a sentence ending with -ing.) A group of words—mainly meteorological

phenomena, such as sun, moon, rain, hail, haze—requires a three-part space before any words of this type can recur. Some of the same words, such as tree/tree and love/love, require a five-part space, and others, such as summer/summer and tears/tears, a seven-part space.

(4) *Rinne* (samsara or recurrence). There are two types of rinne to be avoided: near and distant. A "near" rinne occurs when your description gives a picture more or less similar to the one given by the description preceding the one before you. If "smoke rises" in the eleventh part, you cannot "burn the dead leaves" in the thirteenth part. A "distant" rinne is committed when a combination of similar images in two consecutive parts is repeated elsewhere, even if the pairs occur far apart. So, suppose the eighteenth part describes the moon and the nineteenth, the face of a lover; then you cannot follow someone's description of the moon with one of a lover's face, even if you are twenty, fifty, or seventy parts away from the first combination.

• Optional Rules •

The following rules are optional in that it is up to the participants to adopt them.

FUSHIMONO   The incorporation of a prescribed word or image, called fushimono, in each part of a sequence is a technique I have described earlier (see pages 14–16). The manner of incorporation became complex after Teika; a given item now had to be woven into a part indirectly, rather than directly, so that, if "boat" was a required topic, you had to use a word that would make a word with "boat"—"life," for example—rather than the word "boat" itself or a picture suggestive of one. But by Yoshimoto's time a century later, the technique was being abandoned. In his first treatise on renga, completed in 1345, Yoshimoto said, "Recently, [fushi-mono] is seldom incorporated through a hundred-part sequence." More important, though he listed the technique as one of the rules in that treatise, he dropped it in the definitive version that he completed in 1349. The application of the technique was first reduced to the first eight parts (the "front" of the first sheet), then to the first three, then only to the hokku. It appears that as the incorporation of a word or image became the requirement only of the hokku, it also became an afterthought: a word or image was picked after, not before, the hokku was composed. At the same time, the word or image so picked came to substitute for the title of the sequence.

The decline of the fushimono technique coincided with a growing stress on the content as typified by the ever greater concern with the recurrence of certain words and images within a sequence. Fushimono touched on individual parts and was doomed to be replaced by rules governing the look of the entire sequence. The technique survived long after the fourteenth century, but only as a decoration.

ACROSTIC   Acrostic tanka were fashionable during the Heian period (794–1185). For example, Lady Izumi (born sometime around 976) wrote at least two sequences of thirty-two tanka incorporating lines from a Chinese poem (as read in Japanese translation). The earliest known acrostic in renga form dates from 1165; it incorporates each character of the forty-seven *i-ro-ha* syllabary at the head of each part. The earliest acrostic renga incorporating *i-ro-ha* that remains in its entirety was composed in 1451 by Ichijō Kanera (1402–81), Takayama Sōzei (died 1455), and others. Because it was the fifteenth of the eighth month, when the moon was thought to look the most beautiful in the year, Kanera began:

*I*o nenu ya mizu no monaka no tsuki no aki
In the midwater, the moon, the autumn—have the fish gone
  to sleep?

This was followed by someone whose abbreviated name I cannot identify:

ro *o osu fune no hatsu-kari no koe*
rowing a boat I hear the calls of first geese

Monk Sōzei followed with:

harukanaru kiri-ma no yama wa shima ni nite
harbored in mists a distant mountain looks like an island

and so on. Other than the *i-ro-ha* syllabary, Buddhist prayers seem to have been favored in acrostics.

PALINDROME   As in tanka, palindromes were attempted in
renga. The following links are said to appear toward the end of a set of ten hundred-part sequences composed by Shōtetsu (1381–1459):

na-ka-ba sa-ku ha-gi no so-no ki wa ku-sa-ba ka-na

ki-ku no e-mo na wa ha-na mo-e no ku-ki

Just as the first known palindrome in English ("Lewd I did live, & evil did I dwel") depends on the writing system of the time, so does this set, for *ha/wa* and *ki/gi* are written the same way in the original. And just as in English, palindromes in Japanese tend to be inelegant compositions, their meanings somewhat obscure. In the citation above, the 5-7-5–syllable part is ludicrous, if I understand it correctly, and the 7-7–syllable part does not make sense to me.

I'd like to conclude this chapter by looking at excerpts from a hundred-part renga composed in 1355. In the fourth and fifth months of that year, Gusai and his monk friends visited Yoshimoto, then chancellor, at his mansion and composed ten hundred-part sequences with him and his aides. Of the ten sequences, the first five remain, and the following excerpts are from the very first. Monk Gusai, who was Yoshimoto's teacher and therefore the guest of honor, naturally wrote the hokku:

1 *Na wa takaku koe wa ue nashi hototogisu*　　　　　Gusai
　Highly renowned, the cuckoo's voice cannot be topped

Category: Summer.　Because of its notorious habit of laying eggs in the nests of other birds, the cuckoo has been considered disreputable in the West, meaning "cuckold" in the old days, "insane person" or "simpleton" in more recent American usage. Also, its actual call is described as "fast," "rapid," "busy." Nevertheless, in Japanese poetry the cuckoo has been prized from the beginning as a bird representative of the summer, and its call, especially its "first call," as something eagerly awaited. In renga, the bird is one of the items that may be mentioned only once. Gusai's intention in this hokku is obvious; it is to praise the distinguished host to the skies. The fushimono here is *hito* (person), and when the character for *hito* combined with the one for *na,* it forms a word meaning expert or master, while when combined with the character for *ue,* it forms a word meaning aristocrat. In that too, the hokku exalts Yoshimoto.

2　*shigeru ki nagara mina matsu no kaze*　　　　Yoshimoto
　　lush trees—all of them are pines in a wind

Summer.　Yoshimoto, the host, responds by returning the compliment. All of you, he says, are not only trees with fine foliage, but pine trees at that—the felicitous species that remains green throughout the year. The season is indicated by "lush trees." *Matsu,* here translated pine trees, is a frequently used pun word, also meaning "to wait"; so this part, when taken independently, has the superposed meaning of "all those lush trees wait for a wind," and when linked to the hokku, suggests that "the lush pine trees, as a wind soug　.hrough them, wait for a cuckoo's first call."

3 *yamakage wa suzushiki mizu no nagare nite*　　　　　Eiun
　by the mountain there's a cool water flow

Summer.　Summer is indicated by "cool." The third link
is expected to be a strong turning point, but probably because
this was the very beginning of ten hundred-part sequences, the
poet was cautious enough to choose an approved combination
of "pine tree" and "cool," thereby making the break less than
abrupt. Still, the descriptive focus has moved from midair to
trees, to ground.

4　*tsuki wa mine koso hajime narikere*　　　　　　Shūa
　　the moon is best when at the ridge

Autumn.　The moon, unless modified to mean some other
season, indicates autumn. The seasonal switch is needed because
the maximum three consecutive parts allowed for summer have
been written. The moon here is the one on the fifteenth of the
eighth month, or the "mid-autumn moon," which, as noted
earlier, was thought to present that spherical body in its most
admirable light. The image in the preceding part that makes
this link plausible is the "water flow" that is there to reflect
the moon. The position for the first mention of the moon was
later fixed at the seventh part, but the poet follows the earlier,
more flexible rule that the first moon is to appear somewhere
on the "front" of the first sheet.

5 *aki no hi no ideshi kumoma to mietsuru ni*　　　　Soa
　the autumn sun was just out of the clouds

Autumn.　The weather on an autumn day was thought to
change unpredictably, and the darkness to fall before you knew
it. On its own, this part implies that the sun is again hidden
behind the clouds; but when linked to the preceding part, it
adds that the short autumn day is over and now the moon is
rising.

6   *shigure no sora mo nokoru asa-giri*   Gyōa
     after a shower morning mists remain in the sky

Autumn.   Mists were considered most appropriate for the
autumn and so indicate that season in court poetry. The con-
necting elements are an approved combination of "sunlight
often interrupted by the clouds" and "shower," and the con-
trasting images are "out of the clouds" and "[hidden in the]
mists."

7 *kure goto no tsuyu wa sode ni mo sadamarade*   Mokuchin
  the dew at evening does not settle on my sleeves

Autumn.   This link is technically more elaborate than the
preceding one. It has three words meant to contrast with three
in Gyōa's link: "dew," which is supposed to *fall,* as opposed
to "mists," which are supposed to *rise;* "evening," as opposed
to "morning"; and narrow "sleeves," as opposed to the large
"sky." In addition, the phrase "not to settle" is related to the
"shower," which was thought to be highly restive. The idea of
the link is equally complicated. Because the dew is born of the
restless shower, it does not settle on its prescribed locus, the
sleeves, but instead turns into mists. The word "dew" indicates
that the season is still atutmn.

8   *sato koso kaware koromo utsu koe*   Shigekazu
     in any village there's that sound of beating cloth

Autumn.   Ōe Shigekazu, who wrote this part, was probably
the scribe for this round. Responding to the poetic convention
that the dew on the sleeves is synonymous with tears, he de-
scribes someone on the road, listening to a fulling mallet (see
page 21). The word "any" (the original *kaware* has a more
active verb meaning change) is related to "not settle."
"Sound of beating cloth" specifies the season as autumn. But
with this, the maximum number of five consecutive parts
allowed for autumn has been reached, so the next person must

switch to a different category. Also, with this link ends the formal, "uneventful" front of the first sheet, the *jo* section.

Let us now look at the middle of the sequence where the *ha* section comes to a close and the *kyū* section begins.

45 *ochikochi ni tachi hanaretaru asa-gasumi*   Soa
     far and near, rising separately, the morning hazes

46   *ta ga ie-ie mo haru ya kinu ran*   Eiun
       to all those houses, spring must have come

The patches of haze described in the preceding part are now seen as enveloping separate houses. Spring by the lunar calendar began in the first month of the year.

47 *oiraku no mi ni aratamaru toshi wa nashi*   Gusai
     to me, an aging man, there's no such thing as New Year

48   *kienu bakari no yuki mo itsu made*   Yoshimoto
       the snow just doesn't fade, but until when

49 *tomoshibi no kage o nokoshite fukuru yo ni*   Shūa
     the lamp holds on to its light as night deepens

The category here is "miscellaneous." It is changed to "love" in the next link.

50   *wakaruru hito zo ware o somukuru*   Shigekazu
       parting, she forced me to turn away

But "parting," which makes the link suggestive of love, may also occur to someone who takes to the road. So Gusai describes a traveler.

51 *yuku mama ni ushiro no yama no hedatarite*   Gusai
     I walk ahead, and the mountain behind me goes on receding

52   *tsuki ni mukaeba nokoru hi mo nashi*   Yoshimoto
       I face the moon; nothing remains of the sun

This series of eight parts ending with a description of autumn ("moon"), though picked randomly, may be as lively as any portion of any renga sequence. In the final eight parts, the poets again become formal.

93 *ima komu no aki o wasuruna kaeru kari* Soa
    autumn will come soon—don't forget it, geese, going away

Geese migrate to Japan from Siberia in the fall—in the old days they did so in much more impressive flocks than they do now—and fly away in spring. The season of the description is, therefore, spring.

94 *tsuratsura omoe tsuyu no mi zo kashi* Shūa
    flocks of thoughts—my life is like a dewdrop

The description belongs to the category known as *jukkai*, reflections. Then Shigekazu depicts the leaves falling from a type of vine called *trachelospermum jasminoides,* an evergreen, thereby introducing a winter scene.

95 *kure goto ni chiru ya masaki no tama kazura* Shigekazu
    every evening the vines on spindle trees scatter their leaves

96 *fuyu kakete koso kaze wa samukere* Eiun
    because we're in winter the wind is cold

Though this statement looks innocuous, it too is based on an approved combination of images: "vines in spindle trees" and "wind." Gusai gives it a sharp detail.

97 *o-guruma no waga ato miyuru asa-gōri* Gusai
    I see the ruts of my small cart on the morning ice

98 *futatsu no kawa zo meguri ainuru* Ietada
    the two rivers have come together

Fujiwara no Ietada, Yoshimoto's aide, associates Gusai's two grooves with the two Buddhist rivers—the River of Fire, which symbolizes human resentment, and the River of Water, which symbolizes human greed, in the Buddhist Hell. Between the two is a "white road" that leads to the Pure Land, or Paradise. Yoshimoto, however, interprets the two rivers to mean ones in this world.

99 *Saho-yama no kage yori fukashi Iwa Shimizu*   Yoshimoto
     deeper than the Mount Saho foliage is the Clear-Water-
     through-the-Rocks

The description belongs to the category of *shukugen*, congratulations. The dominant power at court at that time was the Fujiwaras, whose patron deity was enshrined in Nara where Mount Saho is, while the military and de facto ruler of Japan was the Ashikaga clan, whose patron deity was at the Iwa Shimizu (Clear-Water-through-the-Rocks) Hachiman Shrine outside Kyoto. Yoshimoto, as chancellor, was the leader of the Fujiwara family. In concluding the sequence, Monk Gusai extends his congratulations by saying that the trees making up the foliage are two felicitous evergreens: *sakaki* (*cleyera japonica*), whose leafy twigs are used to decorate the shrine, and *tachibana* (*citrus tachibana*), the fragrance of whose flowers is so familiar to court poets:

100   *tokiwa naru ki wa sakaki tachibana.*   Gusai
      the everlasting trees are *sakaki, tachibana.*

~•~ CHAPTER TWO ~•~
Courtly Elegance, Earthy Humor, and Poetry

Essentially a series of contests of wit, renga from the outset tended to move away from elegance, the ideal of court poetry. At the same time, as an outgrowth of the tanka form that in time became the standard vehicle of court poetry, renga tended to be drawn back to the same ideal. As a result, the history of renga is schizophrenic. Wit and its blood relation, humor, existed as strong undercurrents but only occasionally rose to mix with the main stream of elegance as long as court poets remained in top form. When the poets at the court lost vitality and those outside it gained strength, elegance submerged. Still, toward the end of his life as a *haikai* or "humorous" poet, Bashō expressed his mindfulness of the old court ideal by saying that one purpose of his kind of poetry was to "rectify daily language."

Court poetry stultified because the poets made little effort to break away from the rules and restrictions that had accumulated over the centuries. A large part of their inaction was necessitated by the professionalization of poetry writing, and there was therefore little incentive for the poets to seek change. Fujiwara no Tameyo (1251–1338), Teika's great-grandson, said that by his time there were "no sentiments left unsung in the imperial anthologies under various reigns and by the famous poets of various generations," and that one tanka could be different from another only as one face is different from another—each with "two eyes attached to it horizontally, and one nose vertically," but different. Such a defeatist observation came about because, in Tameyo's examples, when you spoke of the cherry blossoms as they came into bloom for the first time in spring, you were required to mistake them for patches of cloud, and when you described the sound of leaves falling, you were supposed to misidentify it as that of a passing shower. Tameyo knew what the problem was, but did nothing except feebly justify living with it.

More or less the same thing happened to renga written by court poets or those who adhered to their poetics. The stultification process as seen in the change from Yoshimoto of the fourteenth century to Monk Shinkei a hundred years later is dramatic. Yoshimoto, the highest court official and the most important preserver of the court's poetic tradition, stressed flexibility and enjoyment, while Shinkei, a non-court poet who regarded renga writing as a means of spiritual and religious discipline, was inflexible and scornful of any notion of enjoyment. (In relation to their social positions their views were the reverse of what might have been expected.) Yoshimoto said that a beginner should learn as much as possible from his teacher but must aim to establish his own style in the end. In contrast, Shinkei argued for absolute servility to one's master, rejecting as unfit to be taught someone who had practiced the art on his own before seeking the guidance of a superior person. Shinkei reasoned that anyone who tainted himself at the outset could not hope to be rectified by the wisest. Yoshimoto thought popularity was the solid ground on which to judge the value of a given style. Fashion has changed four or five times in the past fifty years, he said, and it would be presumptuous for any person, even one considered to be in the know, to challenge the rest of the world in the matter of taste. Shinkei, on the other hand, believed that renga, or any other art for that matter, was beyond the ken of the ordinary mortal. Popularity, in his view, was an aggregate of shallow minds, and to be popular was no honor at all. There have been many men of wisdom who were ignored by their contemporaries and remain unknown, he said.

Would renga composition lead to Buddhist enlightenment? Yoshimoto said yes, that was possible, because "in renga preceding and following thoughts are not connected. Also, the way that the rises and falls, depressing and delightful things, go on shifting from one side to the next, is no different from the way this world is. While you're thinking it was yesterday, today also passes; while you're thinking it's spring, autumn comes; while you're thinking they're [cherry] blossoms, they shift to scarlet leaves—doesn't all this give you the idea that 'blossoms scatter, leaves fall'?" For Yoshimoto renga was first, religion second. For Shinkei it was the other way around. "To learn this way [i.e., renga] and enlighten oneself on the depths of sorrow," he said, "would not be even remotely possible for those who count on living till tomorrow, indulge in various sensuous matters, prize their treasures and, being proud, do not think."

Such observations were based on the two men's opposing views of renga. Laying down comprehensive rules on paper for the first time, Yoshimoto, at age twenty-five, made a point of noting that renga is "a game," and that "easy linking makes good renga." His attitude remained consistent. Toward the end of his life, when he was sixty-three, he said: "No true art is worth anything unless people enjoy it. It's like, for example, folk theater (*dengaku*) or comic theater (*sarugaku*). Renga, too, should be considered well-done while the session maintains fun, only if the session is interesting. No matter how subtle you say [your verse] is, it would be useless if you were clumsy during the session." And, "If it's enjoyable you should even dance." Dancing was unthinkable for Shinkei. Studying renga was to him comparable to "taking Buddhist vows," and once you took up renga, you were expected to meditate on the fact that "both the exalted and the base, the wise and the dumb, will not be breathing by dusk, all being as tenuous as a strand of hair." Naturally he concurred with the dictum of Bontō (1349–1420?): "Renga is renga when done while you are not in a session." Yoshimoto believed that no amount of learning would make a good renga poet but an "utterly ignorant person" could often be good in this game. Shinkei was persistent in condemning those not in the know and relentless in attaching elitist aesthetic import to renga. And while Yoshimoto said tanka and renga were different, Shinkei said they were the same, and his ideals were those of the tanka poets he revered, Teika and his father, Shunzei (1114–1204). Inevitably, renga as practiced by Shinkei and those who held similar views became, like tanka, "a literature for a special class of people," as Fukui Kyūzō put it, and just as court tanka had turned insipid, so in time did court renga.

To illustrate this trend with a sequence that has been admired as "the model" in the genre may be sacrilegious, but the famous *Three Poets at Minase,* written in 1488, has something all too familiar about it and is in the end "monotonous." Let us look at the first eight parts.

1 *Yuki nagara yamamoto kasumu yūbe kana*   Sōgi
   Despite some snow the hill-base is hazy this evening

Category: Spring.   The hokku is by Sōgi because the other two participants, Botange Shōhaku (1443–1527) and Saiokuken Sōchō (1448–1532), were his students. The sequence was composed to be dedicated to the shrine built in memory of the retired emperor Gotoba and his palace at Minase, and in his opening verse Sōgi appropriately alludes to Gotoba's famous tanka commending the view of the area: "As I look out, the hill-base is hazy along Minase River—why did I think the evening was for autumn alone?" (see page 9). The allusion fulfills two requirements of a hokku: place and circumstance of composition. A third requirement, season, is met by the word "hazy." By the lunar calendar the first month, when the three poets sat down and wrote the sequence, marked the beginning of spring.

Kana is a *kireji* (cutting word), which is expected to help the hokku stand on its own by giving the statement a sense of finality. The fushimono here, which substitutes for the title of the sequence, is *hito* (person); combined with a word in the hokku, *yama* (mountain), it forms a word meaning someone who lives on the mountain, such as a woodcutter. (To a degree like the idea of the "noble savage," woodcutters and certain other kinds of people in the wild were considered poetic by Japanese court poets.)

2   *yuku mizu tōku ume niou sato*   Shōhaku
    the water flows distant from a plum-scented village

Spring.   Mindful of Sōgi's allusion, Shōhaku adds a river and, for further detail, a nearer, tangible picture of a village. He himself echoes a tanka by an anonymous poet in the *Kokinshū* (no. 793), which reads:

Minase-gawa arite yuku mizu nakuba koso
tsui ni wagami o taenu to omowame

If Minase River had no water that's there and flows,
I might end up thinking she's abandoned me

The allusion is made to give authority to the use of the phrase, *yuku mizu* (water flows), rather than to enhance the meaning as Sōgi's reference did. The subject of the tanka is love: using the literal sense of *minase-gawa* (dry river), the poet says he would think his lover, who rarely sees him, has abandoned him if water did not occasionally flow in the dry river.

3   *kawakaze ni hito mura yanagi haru miete*   Sōchō
    a river wind, and a stand of willows shows it's spring

Spring.   In contrast to the rather static pictures given by Sōgi and Shōhaku, Sōchō describes a scene with movement. The three images he combines here—wind, willow, spring—are common in tanka on willows, as in Impumon-in no Taifu's (twelfth century) in the *Shin Kokinshū* (no. 73):

Harukaze no kasumi fukitoku taema yori
midarete nabiku aoyagi no ito

In a rift of the haze blown, untangled, by spring winds, turbulent, bending, the strands of green willows

4   *fune sasu oto mo shiruki akegata*   Sōgi
    the sound of a boat being poled, distinct at dawn

Miscellaneous.   Sōgi has been praised for the skill he shows in this link. There is, for one thing, the outstanding description itself. Also, Sōgi suggests that the willows "show" it's spring, because the morning sun makes their green visible. Finally, following the predominantly visual images in the preceding three parts, he brings in an auditory one. Still, the description is solidly based on the following tanka by Fujiwara no Yukiie (dates uncertain) in the *Kin'yōshū* (no. 256):

Kawagiri no tachikometsureba
Takase-bune wakeyuku sao no oto nomi zo suru

Because the river mists rise, filling the air,
only the sound is heard of a Takase boat, its pole being
    plied

5 *tsuki ya nao kiri wataru yo ni nokoruramu*   Shōhaku
  the moon may still linger in the misted-over night

Autumn.   "Mists" is a kigo for autumn, so as if on cue, as it were, Shōhaku begins a description of autumn by using two words that indicate the season, "moon" and "mist." The combination of the two words also has precedent, as in the following tanka by Fujiwara no Kiyosuke (1104–77) in the *Senzaishū* (Collection of Poems for a Thousand Generations, no. 284):

Shiogama no ura fuku kaze ni kiri harete
yasoshima kakete sumeru tsukikage

At the wind blowing over Shiogama Bay the mist clears,
and across the eighty isles the limpid moonlight

The mention of the moon here in the fifth part, rather than in
the seventh, shows that its position was not yet fixed.

6   *shimo oku nohara aki wa kurekeri*   Sōchō
       over the fields where frost has formed, autumn ends

Autumn.   If not qualified as it is here, "frost" indicates
winter. A desolate field and autumn are often paired in court
poetry, as in the following tanka by Prince Tomohira (964–
1009) in the *Shin Kokinshū* (no. 510):

Akikaze ni shioruru nobe no hana yori mo
mushi no ne itaku kare ni keru kana

At autumn winds wilt the flowers out in the field, but far
    worse—
the chirpings of insects have painfully withered

This makes the following part by Sōgi almost predictable:

7 *naku mushi no kokoro tomo naku kusa karete*   Sōgi
     against the chirping insects' hopes the grasses wither

Autumn.   Although the wording of this description is judged
to be excellent, two phrases, "chirping insects" and "grasses
wither," are fixed seasonal indicators, leaving only the middle
section (in the original) to maneuver. The conception itself is
strictly conventional. The eighth part, by Shōhaku, is not much
different:

8   *kakine o toeba arawanaru michi*   Shōhaku
       I come to the fence to visit, the path is exposed

Miscellaneous. This belongs to the category of "miscellaneous" because it has no word or phrase indicating a definite topic. Still, a late autumn scene with insects (crickets, most likely) chirping feebly in the withering grass, as depicted by Sōgi, is expected to provoke in court poetry thoughts of loneliness and yearnings for visits by friends. Witness the following tanka by Fujiwara no Mototoshi (died 1142) in the *Senzaishū* (no. 1090):

Aki hatsuru kareno no mushi no koe taeba
ari ya nashi ya to hito no toekashi

If with autumn ending the insects cease chirping in the withered fields,
I would like someone to visit me to see how I am

These eight parts follow the rule that the opening section of a hundred-part sequence ought to be "uneventful." Six of the eight parts are depictions of landscapes, three of them those of soft-colored spring, three others those of ink-drawn autumn. A human figure appears only in two parts, but in neither too strongly: in the fourth, merely as a suggestion, and in the eighth, more or less as a shadow. The section is executed with finesse and eminently succeeds in creating a world of elegant poetry. But that is precisely the problem. The impression one gets from reading this passage, and the entire sequence, is no different from the impression one gets from reading here and there in an imperial anthology of court poetry.

In addition to his leader's role in this "model" sequence, Sōgi is known as the prime mover in compiling in 1495 the second of the two anthologies of orthodox renga: *Shinsen Tsukubashū* (New Tsukuba Collection). The first, as we have seen, was Yoshimoto's *Tsukubashū* in 1356. But, while Yoshimoto had set aside a section for haikai or "humorous" renga in his anthology, Sōgi did not in his. The reason for Sōgi's decision may have been the great discrepancy that by then existed between orthodox renga and unorthodox *haikai no renga* that probably made him feel it unwise to include both kinds in one selection.

Even so, Sōgi, like Sōchō and Shōhaku, did write the unorthodox kind of renga, and various accounts remain to attest to his quick wit. Sanjōnishi Sanetaka (1455–1537), an aristocratic friend of the three poets, gives an example in his diary. At one gathering in 1499, Sōchō said:

fuji wa sagarite yūgure no sora [7–7]
the wisteria droops against the evening sky

Sōgi promptly followed with:

yoru sariba tare ni kakarite nagusaman [5–7–5]
when night comes, whom will it lie over for consolation?

At this, says Sanetaka, everyone burst out laughing. The diction was that of standard court poetry, but Sōgi's response was risqué.

In the same year an unidentified monk compiled the first known anthology of haikai no renga under the title of *Chikuba Kyōginshū* (Collection of Mad Songs Made on Bamboo Stilts). That was followed a few decades afterward by a far more famous anthology in the same vein, *Inu Tsukubashū* (Dog's Tsukuba Collection). The latter anthology is attributed to the legendary Yamazaki Sōkan, who probably died before 1550. Its initial version is thought to have been put together by the year 1540, when Arakida Moritake (1473–1549) completed his ten hundred-part sequences in the haikai mode, known as *Tobiume Senku* (Flying Plum: Thousand Pieces). Sōkan and Moritake are regarded as the founders of haikai. Unlike the *Chikuba Kyōginshū,* which has been uncovered only recently, Sōkan's *Inu Tsukubashū* was known to the poets of the ensuing centuries, as was Moritake's *Tobiume.* Also, the two works differ from each other. For one thing, Sōkan's anthology, like the three preceding ones, is largely made up of links in the minimum combination of two, which may or may not have been excerpts from longer sequences, whereas Moritake's was planned to be what it is: ten sequences of a hundred parts (plus a celebratory addition half that long and an afterword). For another, the *Inu Tsukubashū* presents haikai in a readily recognizable, earthy manner, whereas *Tobiume* is less hilarious, its haikai chiefly deriving from its rejection of poetic diction.

Let us look at some examples. The first three pairs are for contrast: two elegant tsukeai followed by a humorous one—all dealing with the spring haze. In the *Tsukubashū* is this (no. 10):

taga sode kakete kaze kayōran
whose sleeve has this breeze wafted through?

Sao-hime no kasumi no koromo tachi kasane　　　　　　Tameuji
Princess Sao's robe of haze rises in many layers

What the 7-7–syllable part suggests, by convention, is a fragrance from someone's scented sleeve. In response, Fujiwara no Tameuji (1222–86), Teika's grandson, says the sleeve does not belong to an ordinary mortal, but to the goddess of spring, Princess Sao. In his link *tachi* is a punning word, meaning "to rise" when referring to the haze, and "to cut" when referring to dressmaking; and so is *kasane*, which means "layers" as well as a type of undergarment.

In the *Shinsen Tsukubashū*, Monk Sōzei has the following:

ura ka omote ka koromo tomonashi
inside or outside, I cannot tell of that robe

shinonome no ashita no yama no usu-gasumi　　　　　　Sōzei
against the eastern clouds the morning hills are veiled with haze

As is shown in the preceding pair, spring hazes used to be compared to robes for mountains. Sōzei here says he cannot tell whether he's looking at the inside or the outside of the robe because the day has not fully broken. In the *Inu Tsukubashū*, such elegant affectations are given a rude jolt:

kasumi no koromo suso wa nurekeri
the robe of haze is wet at its hem

Sao-hime no haru tachi nagara shito o shite
Princess Sao of spring pissed as she started

The *maeku* (initial part) is innocuous enough; but, instead of
explaining conventionally why the robe is wet, the respon-
dent—it could have been Sōkan—says it is because the goddess
of spring inopportunely succumbed to the call of nature.

The additional examples from the *Inu Tsukubashū* that follow
may show one way that haikai no renga was different from
orthodox renga in the court tradition.

his gentle thoughts—no, I can't say that

a brush-maker admires a wild cherry, as he passes by it

The bark of a wild cherry called *kabazakura* was good material
for brushes, so a brush-maker stopping to admire it is, when
you think about it, suspect.

~

though in a dream it must hurt

asleep on a flower the butterfly was struck by raindrops

This tsukeai is understandable as it is, but may become more
interesting when one is reminded of the well-known passage in
Chuang Tzu: "Once Chuang Chou dreamt he was a butterfly,
a butterfly flitting and fluttering around, happy with himself
and doing as he pleased. He didn't know he was Chuang Chou.
Suddenly he woke up and there he was, solid and unmistakable
Chuang Chou. But he didn't know if he was Chuang Chou who
had dreamt he was a butterfly, or a butterfly dreaming he was
Chuang Chou." There is also a pun: the original word for
"asleep" also means "wet."

~

ELEGANCE, HUMOR, AND POETRY · 53

A hokku:

It's all gone! this indeed is a snow Buddha

The reference is to the Buddhist teaching that life is transient. The original word for "snow Buddha," *yuki-botoke,* contains a near homophonic pun, suggesting a meaning, "the snow too has melted."

~

pain in the ass gets worse, so does hunger

a pity—the baby monkey can't get the bur off the chestnut!

The Japanese monkey, a macaque, has a red face and red posterior. Here, the redness of the posterior is thought to have resulted from its owner's sitting on a tree too long.

~

she spreads her net everywhere

Queen Anne I adore has captured my garden with her lace

In case the reader is puzzled by the sudden appearance of Queen Anne, the original goes: *doko to mo iwazu chigiri koso sure / hizō suru niwa no kusahana kohimegoze.*

~

a house built, but it's so fragile

a spider has spanned its web across plantain leaves

The leaves of the plantain, *bashō,* tear easily. (Most likely it was this attribute of the plant that Bashō had in mind when he saw the plant given him grow so well and adopted its name as his pen name.)

~

A hokku:

Monkey's ass: immune to the tree-searing wind, maple-crimson

The macaque is one of the few monkeys that live above the snow line.

~

I get only nuts for my drinks

and all these young men have ugly faces

Homosexuality and male prostitution were common topics in popular literature.

~

arm for a pillow he keeps listening

quite late on his wedding night a cuckoo calls

Someone lying with his arm for a pillow suggests a listless person. The respondent confounds that expectation by giving another meaning of "arm for a pillow," which is "to sleep with someone."

~

loving someone out of reach—what a pity!

hugging a young man far taller than himself

~

all his tender thoughts must lie in one hole

a rat carried off her love letter this evening

~

An example with two *tsukeku* (linked parts):

holding the paper to wipe it with and crying, crying

the sword handed down by his father, now all rusty

time for the novice to take vows, and this is the blade

In the second link the blade is for shaving the head of the novice, signaling his decision to enter priesthood.

~

And here's the most famous piece from the *Inu Tsukubashū*:

upsetting, but funny too

even when my parent lay dying, I kept farting

The haikai as exemplified by these samples represents what the word originally meant: humor. But Moritake gave a broader meaning to the term by questioning humor as its sole property. "Should haikai be thoughtless, intended only to make people laugh?" he asked, and suggested that his renga were haikai because of their inclusion of "locally used daily language" and "sentiments and expressions that have become personal." A century later, when attempts were made to distinguish haikai no renga from orthodox renga, this inclusion of "daily language" (*zokugo, zokugen*), diction not allowed in court poetry, was repeatedly singled out as the principal feature of haikai. Typical may be the observation in the *Haikai Shogaku Shō* (Haikai Primer), published in 1641 by Saitō Tokugen (1559–1647), that haikai is "renga with daily language added," and that the first of the "five superior pleasures" of haikai is its "use of daily language."

The opening section of the first sequence in Moritake's *Tobiume* reads:

1 *Tobiume ya karogaroshiku mo kami no haru*
   The Flying Plum is feather-light in this Deity's spring

2   *ware mo ware mo no karasu uguisu*
    "Me too, me too," follow crows, warblers

3 *nodokanaru kaze fukurō ni yama miete*
   when a peaceful wind 'owls over the hills I see

Tobiume (Flying Plum) refers to a legend about Sugawara no Michizane, who was exiled at the pinnacle of his court career. According to the legend, when leaving his mansion in Kyoto, he composed a farewell poem for his favorite plum tree; thereupon, the tree flew to the place where its "master" was condemned to spend the rest of his life. The poem was:

Kochi fukaba nioi okose yo ume no hana
aruji nashi tote haru o wasuru na

When the eastwind blows, send over your fragrance, plum
    blossoms;
even without your master, do not forget spring

Moritake made this reference because the twenty-fifth of the
first month of 1536, when he began work on the ten hundred-
part sequences, was the anniversary of the death of Michizane,
the patron deity of renga.

The words and phrases not considered "poetic" in this
section are *karogaroshiku* (feather-light), *ware mo ware mo* (me
too, me too), *karasu* (crow), and *fukurō* (owl). The haikai of the
section also derives from the nimble use of wordplay. In the
hokku, *tobi* means "flying" and "kite" (the bird), the latter
triggering the mention of crows and warblers in the wakiku;
kami (deity) also means "paper," which makes it a natural
word to follow "feather-light"; and *kami no haru* (deity's
spring) comes close to meaning "pasting up paper," which
makes "me too, me too" natural and funny. The daisan uses
the kind of pun not often used in English: *fuku* of the word
fukurō (owl) also means "to blow," enabling the word to
function as a verb and a noun.

The third sequence begins:

1 *Hana yori mo hana ni arikeru nioi kana*
   Fragrance is not so much in the blossoms as in the nose

2   *tsuki wa oboro ni fukuru inoshishi*
      moon opaque, it grows late over the wild boar

3 *haru no yo no yume ya sanagara ushi naran*
   this spring night his dreams must be all bull

The haikai of this section comes from the generally earthy tone
of its descriptions, in addition to the use of patently unpoetic
words, such as "nose." Its humor lies in the juxtaposition of
elegant and inelegant images: "blossoms," "fragrance,"
"moon opaque (hazy)" and "spring night dreams," set along-

side "nose," "wild boar," and "bull." Puns also play a role. The hokku has two words that are homophonic: *hana,* the first time, means "blossom," and the second time, "nose"—the latter prompting the association of a wild boar rooting with its singular snout. The wild boar, in turn, is related to the pun in the daisan, *ushi,* which means "bull," as well as "depressing."

Moritake could be coarse rather in the manner of the *Inu Tsukubashū.* In the fifth sequence the following links occur:

8 *Shigehira kai o fukare nuru nari*

9 *furo ni iru Senju no mae no kayuku shite*

Shigehira (1156–84) was a general of the Taira clan captured alive in a crucial battle with the Minamoto clan. Though he was eventually executed, the head of the Minamoto, Yoritomo (1147–99), treated him politely, at one time sending Senju (1165–88), one of his maids, to console him. The meeting between the general and the maid occurs in a bathroom where she comes in to wash him. That night they play music to each other. Learning of his execution, Senju becomes a nun and soon afterward dies. The story, told in *The Tale of the Heike,* became the basis of *Senju,* an affecting Noh play attributed to Komparu Zenchiku (1405–68).

So, the eighth part, following the part suggesting someone "captured alive," means, "Shigehira has blown on his conch shell." But because the word *kai* (shellfish) sometimes refers to the female sexual organ, and the word *fuku* (to blow) also means "to wipe," the eighth part can mean, "Shigehira has wiped her shellfish." It is this second meaning that is used for the following line, which, at one level, means, "taking a bath, Senju had an itch on her front."

The sentiments and expressions used in this pair of links are totally alien to court poetry and therefore totally haikai, although Moritake did not frequently indulge in this mode of humor. In any event, if Sōkan reaffirmed the importance of the sense of earthy playfulness in renga, Moritake recognized and enunciated the importance of the use of daily language and the world it describes. In this respect, what he did in *Tobiume* is comparable to what Wordsworth did in *Lyrical Ballads*.

For all their worth, Sōkan's *Inu Tsukubashū* and Moritake's *Tobiume* did not at once usher in a new age. Another hundred years had to pass before haikai was taken seriously and a large number of haikai collections and treatises on the genre started appearing. During that time renga poets of the traditional school remained productive and influential. For example, Satomura Jōha (1524–1602), a dominant figure in the sixteenth century, is believed to have taken part in at least five thousand renga sessions, and his descendants went on to hold the hereditary right to provide the Tokugawa shogunate with official instructors.

From the times of Sōkan and Moritake to the 1670s, when Bashō came on the scene, two men helped push haikai forward: Matsunaga Teitoku (1571–1653) and Nishiyama Sōin (1605–82). A tanka poet and classical scholar with encyclopedic knowledge, Teitoku set rules and standards for haikai, although what he mainly did was to relax the existing ones intended for orthodox renga. Through his prestige, his Confucian rectitude, and his own compositions, he also gave respectability to the genre. In doing so, however, he made haikai rule-bound and short on playfulness. It was against this tendency of his school, known as Teimon, that the people who gathered around Sōin rebelled. These people, later to be known as Danrin, demanded freedom in technique and spirit. Sōin was a professional renga poet of the old school and his sally into the genre was never wholehearted; he announced withdrawal from it in the end when he felt those claiming bondage under his leadership were going too far. Still, his casual approach and his imaginative linking technique brought back liveliness and fun to haikai. Bashō, who took part in a renga session with Sōin in 1675, when Sōin's fame was at its peak, later described him as the "restorer/

founder" (*chūkō kaizan*) of the kind of haikai he and his friends wrote.

Teitoku's moralistic approach is well reflected in his condemnation of the best-known piece in the *Inu Tsukubashū*. It appears in the "Yodo-gawa" section of his *Shinzō Inu Tsukubashū* (New and Enlarged Dog's Tsukuba Collection, 1643), where he adds third links to the tsukeku of Sōkan's anthology, with comments, mostly on his own compositions:

upsetting, but funny too

even when my parent lay dying, I kept farting

"Even for haikai it is not proper to shame one's father or mother. Not to mention Confucianism, Buddhism also forbids unfilial behavior. In addition, even disregarding the five syllables [i.e., *he o kokite*, 'I kept farting'], is there anything that is not upsetting at someone's death? Why did not the editor revise it before putting it in? If you do not regard renga, haikai, and all, to say nothing of tanka, as means of teaching people, it will do no good to you, no matter how much honor you may gain. If this link said at least 'someone else's parent,' its effect might be superior. If it is one's own parent, how could it possibly be funny? Anyone who could think it funny would not be born of a human; he would be inferior to a beast. Unless you carefully consider this sort of thing, you will be derided by later people and deemed inferior to those who do not dabble in haikai."

Then Teitoku goes on to add his third link:

nochinochi neko no toru wa ko-itachi
later on the cat will get the baby weasel

(In writing this link, Teitoku takes the word *waga*, a focal point of his denunciation, to mean "its" or "his," rather than "my." With his link, he suggests that it was a baby weasel that farted while its parent was being devoured by a cat. In his judgment morality evidently did not extend to weasels.)

What Teitoku found upsetting in the tsukeku is disrespect for filial piety, the foundation of Confucian philosophy. He did not feel as strongly about indecencies. For example, in the "Aburakasu" section of the same book, where he writes his tsukeku to the maeku of Sōkan's anthology, he has the following among his eleven tsukeku to "upsetting, but funny too":

hitonaka de korobu onago no mae dashite
a woman fell among the people, baring her front

Mostly, though, he was genteel, as may be seen in one of the three tsukeku he added to "the robe of haze is wet at its hem":

tennin ya amakudarurashi haru no umi
a heavenly being must have descended from the sky to the spring
   sea

Teitoku may have formed his genial approach partly from the company he kept, which to a large extent consisted of scholars, poets, generals, and noblemen. "Even for haikai," he said in his *Tensui Shō* (Heavenly Water, 1644?), "you should not do anything base." Although a good poet can make something attractive from something base, a bad one tends to make something attractive base. So, "young beginners," especially, must avoid, "in front of noblemen and court ladies, dealing with talk of the lower part of the body, names of base food items, rice, money, and business gains and losses."

Teitoku's main linking technique was kotoba-zuke, linking through demonstrably related words and phrases. The following is the opening section of a hundred-part renga, known as *Uta Izure* (Which Sings Better), which he wrote around 1624 and later annotated for the benefit of his students.

1 *Uta izure Komachi Odori ya Ise Odori*
   Which sings better? Komachi Dance or Ise Dance?

Category: Autumn.   The Komachi Dance became popular in and around Kyoto at the beginning of the Edo Period (1603–1868). Ono no Komachi, a poet of the mid-ninth century, was reputed to have been such a beauty that her name became synonymous with a beautiful young woman. The dance was danced by the prettiest girls of the town on the seventh of the seventh month, the day the Princess Weaver (the star Vega) and the Oxherd (the star Altair), the ill-fated lovers of Chinese legend, have a once-a-year meeting in the River of Heaven (the Milky Way). The girls sang as they danced through the streets. The Ise Dance, originating in the province of Ise, was for the fifteenth of the seventh month, the day marking the Bon Festival intended for the appeasement of the souls of the dead. This dance, too, became popular about the same time. It happens that Ise is the name of another early woman poet, who died in 939. Teitoku explains that he intended this hokku, by way of indirect reference to the two poets, to express his admiration for them, "both so good that one can't tell who is the better."

2   *doko no Bon ni ka oryaru Tsurayuki*
      whose Bon has that Tsurayuki?

Autumn. Ki no Tsurayuki, a well-known male poet of about the same time (c.868–c.946), is invoked to decide who is the better poet of the two. Because the three poets are all dead, what is implied is: At whose house is Tsurayuki staying when Komachi and Ise are dancing right here? The linking is based on strict word association: Komachi—Ise—Tsurayuki, and [Bon] Dance—Bon. "Tsurayuki" may also be a pun meaning, "Where's that face?"

3 *sora ni shirarenu yuki furu wa tsukiyo nite*
   In the sky falls unfamiliar snow: a moonlit night

Autumn. This alludes to Tsurayuki's tanka in the *Shūishū* (no. 64):

   Sakura chiru ki no shitakaze wa samukarade
   sora ni shirarenu yuki zo furikeru

The wind under cherry trees as petals scatter is not cold,
but in the sky unfamiliar snow is falling

The poem is based on the literary affectation of confusing falling cherry blossoms with untimely snowflakes. The season it describes is spring, but Teitoku switches it to autumn by suggesting that the confusing element was not cherry blossoms falling en masse, but the bright light of the full moon of the seventh month. The scene of the hokku also changes—from daytime to night. Teitoku says part of the haikai of this link lies in its unusual syllabic breakup: normally it should be 5-7-5, but here it is 7-5-5. A modern reader may be reminded of Bashō's hokku noted for its equally unusual syllabic pattern of 5-5-7:

Umi kurete kamo no koe honokani shiroshi
The sea darkens, and the voices of ducks faintly white

Here again Teitoku's linking is through straight word association: introducing Tsurayuki's poem after mentioning the poet.

4   *itsu mo nezama ni dasu kome no ii*
    a meal of rice always served when he's ready for bed

Miscellaneous. Teitoku notes there was a saying among novices that rice served on moonlit nights was one thing one never tired of. White rice is set aside another white object, snow.

5 *nage hōru sushi no hara mo ya akinuran*
  thrown out—the belly of the *sushi* must have split open

Miscellaneous. The *sushi* here is the kind made by filling gutted fish with rice. One meaning—or the meaning the translation is meant to suggest—is that a rich kid described in the preceding link (a novice's dream come true) is so spoiled with good food he carelessly tosses aside a delicacy offered him. The puns are somewhat complex. *Akinuran,* here translated "must have split open," also means "must be tired of," enabling the tsukeku to suggest something like "he threw off the *sushi,* he must be tired of it.'' Then too, Teitoku says *nezama,* here translated ''when he's ready for bed,'' is closely related to *nage hōru,* here translated ''thrown out,'' in that the word also means the posture of something thrown out and lying flat on its side. Associating ''a meal of rice'' with ''*sushi*'' is logical.

6   *oke mochinagara korobu ōnoke*
       carrying a tub, he fell flat on his back

Miscellaneous. According to Teitoku, ''thrown out,'' which in the preceding part refers to the *sushi,* now describes the tub containing it. *Sushi* and tub are yet another example of demonstrable association.

7 *suberurashi mizukumi-michi no nobori-zaka*
    must be slippery—the uphill path for getting water

Miscellaneous. As Teitoku says, ''fell flat on his back'' prompts the image of an ''uphill path.'' The connection of ''tub'' and ''getting water'' is again explicit.

8   *taki goranji ni izuru in-sama*
       to see a cascade Mr. Retired Emperor has come out

Miscellaneous. Teitoku explains that *suberu* in the preceding part is taken here to mean ''to slip from the throne'' or ''to abdicate,'' thereby making possible the introduction of a ''retired emperor.'' The two links suggest a retired emperor who now has enough leisure and freedom to take an un-imperial path to go to see a natural spectacle. ''Getting water'' and ''cascade'' are obviously related as water images. The switch in imagery is from a commoner, who has to get water from its source whenever he needs it, to an exalted person who doesn't have to worry about such humble matters.

In contrast to the linking technique of kotoba-zuke that Teitoku and his followers used, Sōin and those who regarded him as their leader favored kokoro-zuke, in which the response is not to any specific words but to the general sentiment of the preceding part. Because the two techniques, like all others, are essentially based on association, the difference between them should not be overemphasized. Nevertheless, the stress on words and phrases in kotoba-zuke is evident from a string of manuals published by the more outspoken members of the Teimon school—books listing words and phrases with those that may be legitimately used in association with them. Both the lemmas and the words and phrases to be associated with them in these volumes quickly increased.

To illustrate the Danrin's move away from the Teimon in linking technique would be difficult, were it not for the vigorous charges and countercharges exchanged between the two schools (and often within each school). One such exchange occurred when, in early 1674, Sōin published a solo sequence of one hundred parts, called *Kabashira* (A Column of Mosquitos). In its afterword he modestly said that the sequence had as much worth as "the grass that soothes me as I sit alone in my grass hut," and that, now at age seventy, he no longer cared whether people would "forgive or disparage" him. At once, a monk, anonymous but evidently of the Teimon school, decided to disparage him; in a booklet entitled *Shibu Uchiwa* (A Conservative's Fan), he ridiculed the sequence part for part. Sōin was annoyed and wrote an indirect response, asserting in effect that he had the right to do whatever he pleased. But he did not make it public until six years later. Instead, it was Okanishi Ichū (1639–1711), a leading critic and poet of his school, who published in the following year a part-by-part rebuttal called *Shibu Uchiwa Hentō* (Response to A Conservative's Fan). Let us look at the criticism and the response to it in some detail.

1 *Kabashira wa ogakuzu sasō yūbe kana*
  A column of mosquitos invites sawdust this evening

Summer. As the anonymous monk notes, *kabashira* is a swarm of mosquitos that often gather in summer evenings, and *ogakuzu* here refers to the sawdust that used to be burned to repel the insect. Unfortunately, the monk misquotes the first five syllables as "Kabashira *ni*," which changes the meaning of the hokku to "This evening invites sawdust to a column of mosquitos." As a result, his complaint is invalid that he "can't understand this hokku," and that if it's supposed to make sense, the description is "inadequate." Ichū, in his rebuttal, repeats the misquote and compounds the problem, but he says one notable thing: referring to *Haikai Mōgyū* (Haikai Meng Ch'iu), a general introduction to haikai he published in the previous year, he asserts that in haikai anything goes, because "true haikai" means "unfettered freedom." (In this same book, Ichū rejects Teitoku's argument against "upsetting, but funny too / even when my parent lay dying, I kept farting" on the ground that Teitoku's moral reasonings, though "honest and sincere," belong to "tanka and renga of the old school," not to haikai.)

2   *kawaki sunago no niwa no suzukaze*
     over the dry sand in the garden, a cool wind

Summer. The monk complains that if there is a "cool wind," no mosquitos will gather. In addition, he says, nothing in the hokku justifies the introduction of "dry sand." Because of the story in *Tsurezuregusa* (Essays in Idleness) by Yoshida Kenkō (1282–1350) where a true gentleman is said to prepare dry sand rather than sawdust for the wet ground (episode 177), "sawdust" may be intended to be the connecting element of "dry sand," the monk says, but "here it is hard to make the connection." In defense, Ichū says yes, the story in *Tsurezuregusa* is indeed meant to link the waki to the hokku. Furthermore, can anything top the "superb combination" of "dry sand" and "cool wind"? As for the argument that mosquitos don't gather in the wind, that is nonsense. Why, there is a Chinese "poem on mosquitos" that says they gather "despite the wind."

3   *sakè hitotsu nodo tōru ma ni tsuki idete*
     while a shot of sakè passes the throat, the moon appears

Autumn. The monk expresses amazement at the "speedy advent of the moon." Citing the idea of *hon'i,* which was developed and elaborated by court poets, that any poetic object must be described as if it had only one "true" attribute, he says the hon'i of the moon is that it is something one is supposed to wait for, as witness a tanka by the retired emperor Sanjō (976–1017) in the *Shin Kokinshū* (no. 382):

Ashibiki no yama no anata ni sumu hito wa
matade ya aki no tsuki o miruran

Those who live beyond the foot-wearying mountain—
do they see the autumn moon without waiting so?

This is the sort of attitude one ought to bring to the moon, the monk says; compared with this, the idea Sōin describes in his line is "upsetting." In response, Ichū says the monk is addressing haikai from the viewpoint of renga of the old school; the daisan is perfectly linked to the waki through "dry" / "while a shot of sakè passes the throat," and "cool wind" / "moon." As for the overall cast of the link, the idea that "time flies" (although the sun and the moon may seem "loitering" to the monk) has been supported by Chinese "horoscopers, Confucianists, and Buddhists."

The monk and Ichū go on in a similar vein. The monk complains that Sōin often fails to provide linking elements, and that those he does provide do not meet the established standards. Ichū, on the other hand, finds linking elements in most cases and, when he can't, taunts the monk for his failure to understand what haikai is all about. For justification or for making a point, the monk most often turns to traditional tanka, whereas Ichū refers to Chinese sources.

Here is the middle section of *Kabashira:*

48   *nōte kanawanu tabi no suitō*
     you can't do without a canteen when traveling

49 *hanazakari tabako ni kiseru uma ni kura*
    flowers at their prime: tobacco and a pipe, on the horse a
    saddle

The forty-eighth part describes a traveler. When linked to the forty-ninth part, the description becomes that of someone who has come to see the cherry blossoms in full bloom. The forty-ninth part alludes to a tanka of Minamoto no Yorimasa (1104–80), as quoted in somewhat different form in the Noh play *Kurama Tengu* (Goblin of Kurama):

> *Hana sakaba tsuge yo to iishi yamamori no*
> *kuru oto su nari uma ni kura oke*

I said to the hill-keeper, "Tell me when the flowers
    bloom";
now I hear the sound of him coming. Put the saddle on the
    horse!

The allusion here, intended to justify the combination of cherry flowers and a saddled horse, gives a twist to the elegant atmosphere of the original tanka by adding the alien objects of tobacco and a pipe. Referring to the forty-eighth part, the anonymous monk sneers that "can't do without" linked with "tobacco," "canteen" with "flowers at their prime," and "traveling" with "horse" must be too much of a "load" for a "feeble horse." Ichū retorts that this considerable load is "quite an accomplishment for recent times."

50 *yari-ume ippon sate zōri tori*
    a single lance plum, and here's a sandal bearer

Spring. The monk finds a "lance plum" set aside a "sandal bearer" interesting, but wonders who is to have the "tobacco" and the "pipe," because it is unreasonable to expect the sandal bearer to have them. Ichū dismisses the monk's puzzlement, saying the picture is as vivid "as if actually seen."

51 *haru wa kinu rōnin naredo nandoki mo*
  spring has come; though masterless, at any time

Spring. This part, with the preceding one, alludes to the story told in the Noh play *Hachi no Ki* (Potted Trees). The story concerns a poor warrior living in adversity who warms a wayward traveler in heavy snow by burning his cherished potted trees, a plum among them. He tells the traveler—in fact the most powerful man of the land and the warrior's lord traveling incognito—that despite his sorry state he would respond to a call to arms at any time. Later he keeps his word and receives ample reward for his sacrifice and loyalty. The monk faults this part on several counts. His principal charge is that the phrase, "at any time," doesn't make sense without the preceding part, and that even then it doesn't have a linking element in it. In reply, Ichū manages to duck the charge by making an important point: a phrase does not necessarily have to have a connecting element if it can be justified by the overall sentiment of the preceding part.

52 *kami sakayaki o soru bakari nari*
  all he needs is barber's work

Miscellaneous. My translation here is relatively free because the original is ambiguous enough to suggest a variety of meanings. Read both alone and with the fifty-first part in mind, it seems to refer to the peculiar hairdo of the Japanese male during the Edo period and may mean something like "he is ready (or has only) to dress up his hair, shave his crown." The monk complains that it is not clear, and that, whatever its intended meaning, it cannot be linked to the preceding part. Ichū replies that the fifty-first and fifty-second parts, if read together with a stress on "at any time," readily make sense.

53 *kokoro yasuki hōkō naraba kono machi ni*
  "If it's easy employment, I'd like to stay in this town"

Miscellaneous. The monk suggests that if the fifty-second part is intended to mean, as it may, "I can only do barber's work," then the two parts must describe a barber employed by a town, and the fifty-third part must be a request made by such a person. Still, he finds no connecting element, and points out that someone looking for a job can't be introduced in a sequence when an unemployed warrior is mentioned only two parts back. Ichū says the monk is right in saying this part is a request, a remark. As for the monk's complaint pointing to a violation of a rule, Ichū argues, with a citation from a Chinese poem, that a masterless warrior is someone in an adverse condition, not necessarily someone seeking employment.

54   *ginsu ika hodo nozomi naruran*
    "I wonder how much he would want"

Miscellaneous.   The monk says someone getting a new job "may depend on an advance," but a renga part shouldn't depend on the preceding part. His complaint is based on his interpretation of the line as meaning, "I wonder how much they'd pay me," in which case the two parts are too close. Ichū replies that the line is meant to be a remark by a third party, not by the person who made the preceding remark. He then scolds the monk for his inability to understand the grammar of the line.

The last two parts deal with the subject matter that Sōin and his followers excelled in describing: daily activities of ordinary people. The opening section of the hundred-part sequence Sōin wrote in response to the anonymous monk's criticism shows this plebeian aspect of Danrin haikai in an even more pronounced way.

The column of mosquitos—if to be planed, just one shave

   away from orders, bottle gourd and an inn

I see lots of melons, eggplants bought by bidding

   "Bargains! Bargains!" thin blades, vegetable knives

he pretends to strip and disembowel himself

   cleverly disposing of all debts

The hokku is a wry response to the anonymous monk's elaborate criticism: a column of mosquitos, of course, can't be planed. The waki suggests a carpenter who, taking the hokku to be an order from his superviser, realizes it's the end of the day and looks out from the construction site they are working on. The bottle gourd, or *yūgao,* puts on flowers that bloom in the evening and wilt in the morning. The daisan changes the scene to morning by describing a vegetable shop that has just brought in fresh produce from a predawn market. The fourth part continues the description of the same shop but changes the focus from produce to lively shop-hands. In the next part the scene changes from a vegetable shop to a cutlery store, though the focus remains on the people selling their wares; here, a man comically shows that the knife the customer is interested in is sharp enough for a ritual disembowelment. In the sixth part the man changes to someone deep in debt but clever enough to convince his creditor through his gesture that his pecuniary adversity does not allow payment of the monies owed.

From these examples it may be seen that Teitoku's lines are laborious compared with Sōin's, and that Sōin's technique is to move the sequence onward by the general sense conveyed in the preceding part. Bashō, who first studied with a follower of Teitoku, became an ardent student of Danrin haikai with its emphasis on "freedom" in linking and realism in description. He then tried some new approaches and in the end established his own style of linked poetry that went beyond both courtly elegance and earthy humor.

In 1677, when he was still under the strong influence of Danrin, Bashō composed a sequence of a hundred parts with Yamaguchi Sodō (also Shinshō, 1642–1716) and Itō Shintoku (1633–98). It begins:

1 *Ara nan tomo naya kinō wa sugite fukuto-shiru* Bashō
  Look, nothing has happened! Yesterday passed after the
    blowfish soup

2   *samusa shisatte ashi no saki made*   Sodō
    the chill goes down to the tip of the toe

3   *iainuki arare no tama ya midasuran*   Shintoku
    the sword, drawn, might disturb the hailstones

4   *sessha myōji wa Kaze no Shinohara*   Bashō
    "My surname is Kaze no Shinohara"

Some species of blowfish are highly prized as food but carry
lethal poison in their intestines. In the hokku, Bashō expresses
relief in finding himself not poisoned by the blowfish soup he
ate; to do so, he uses a stock exclamation in Noh plays, *"ara
nan tomo naya,"* which in its original use conveys a sense of
disappointment. So the humor of the hokku lies in coupling a
highbrow allusion to Noh drama with a lowbrow matter of food
poisoning and in using a well-known phrase in an unusual sense.
Sodō, in his waki, describes one of the good effects of taking a
nonlethal dose of blowfish poison: improved blood circulation.
This effect is then interpreted by Shintoku to be a description
of a drug sold by a street-vendor, who does swordplay to attract
a crowd. Such a swordplayer-vendor customarily introduced
himself at the beginning of a session: hence, Basho's fourth link.
The element that connects the third part to the fourth is a
famous tanka by Minamoto no Sanetomo (1192–1219) de-
scribing a warrior in hail. That, as well as the formality of Bashō's
phrasing, enables the fourth part to suggest a warrior. (And that
suggestion is indeed taken up in the fifth part.) The linking
proceeds with ease, the interpretation differing at each turn.

Alluding to a passage or a theme of a Noh play in an ironic
manner, as Bashō's hokku above does, was fashionable for quite
a while among haikai poets, but allusion in general was a per-
manent tool for them. A dramatic example is the hokku on
which Ezra Pound built imagism, especially his notion of
"superposition":

The fallen blossom flies back to its branch:
    A butterfly.

72 · FROM RENGA TO HAIKU

This translation, quoted by Pound in two lines, is given in three lines and in slightly different form by his imagist friend, F. S. Flint, so Pound may have made changes to suit his purpose. The original, attributed to Moritake, seems to have little to do with imagism or superposition:

Rakka eda ni kaeru to mireba kochō kana
A fallen blossom returned to its branch, I thought—it was a
  butterfly!

Aside from the conceit of mistaking a butterfly for a fallen blossom, the hokku relies for its humor on the saying, "A fallen blossom doesn't return to its branch," which, in turn, is a paraphrase of part of a couplet in Chinese in the *Zenrin Kushū* (A Zen Phrase Anthology, 1574):

The broken mirror will not shine again;
the fallen blossom can hardly return to the branch.

(A twist of this type must be common in any literature. A good specimen in the English language is, I am told, the following: "And after many a summer dies the duck." In Tennyson's *Tithonus* the last word is "swan.")
  Some twists in allusion are subtler. Take the following hokku, which Bashō wrote in 1688:

Hototogisu kieyuku kata ni shima hitotsu
A cuckoo fades away, and in its direction, a single island

This alludes to a tanka by Fujiwara no Sanesada (1130–91) in the *Senzaishū* (no. 161):

Hototogisu nakitsuru kata o nagamureba
tada ariake no tsuki zo nokoreru

A cuckoo called, and I looked in that direction;
there only the daybreak moon was left

Here the allusion is intended, on the one hand, to enlarge the imagery of the hokku by recalling the world suggested by the tanka and, on the other, to create a sort of humor by making short shrift of what has been described as "tanka-esque lyricism." The effect of such short shrift may be compared to that of a fussy stylist's rewrite of a long-winded official announcement.

About a year after composing the hokku that begins "Look, nothing has happened! . . . " that is cited earlier, Bashō became a sōshō, master. This designation referred to someone who presided over a renga session or to someone formally given permission by a particular school to collect fees as a renga teacher. In Bashō's case becoming a sōshō probably meant he began collecting money for his instructions. Evidently he did well, getting many poems published in notable collections of the period and promoting the writings of those who studied with him. But in a few years the Danrin mode of haikai reached its peak and began declining rapidly. In 1681 Bashō wrote to Takayama Biji (1649–1718): "Those supposed to be sōshō still indulge in the haikai of three or four years ago, most looking dated, so that those who study with them are worse still, lost as to haikai." In the preceding year he had become skeptical enough of what he was doing, professionally and philosophically, to move his living quarters from the middle of the city of Edo to a village on its periphery, Fukagawa. He expressed his feelings at that time in his earliest known piece of *haibun,* prose written in a haikai spirit.

Brushwood Door

After living in destitution in the city for nine years, I moved to live near Fukagawa. "Ch'ang-an from times past's a place for fame and profit; | empty-handed, no money, it's hard for me to get along here." I now think the person who said this wise, probably because I am poor:

A gust rakes tea, its leaves, to my brushwood door

The quoted poet is Po Chü-yi. The next haibun, probably written during the winter of 1681, shows that Bashō regarded himself as a hermit of sorts, while reading Chinese poets and trying to write like them as much as was possible in the short hokku form:

THE OLD MAN THE BEGGAR

Framed in the window: the thousand-autumn snows of the west ranges; tied up by the gate: boats come ten thousand miles from the eastern sea.

I knew this verse, but did not see its heart; fathomed its desolation, but did not know its pleasure. The only thing in which I excel old Tu Fu is in the number of illnesses. Hiding behind the plantain of my quiet and simple thatched hut, I call myself the old man the beggar.

Sound of paddles slapping the waves, my bowels freeze tonight,
  and the tears

At Poor Mountain the pot cries out at the frost, its voice cold

  "Buying Water"

Ice bitter, I moisten my mole throat

  "Year-end"

Darkening, darkening—with rice cakes my echoes, I lie alone

The two lines quoted at the beginning of the haibun are the last two from a quatrain by Tu Fu (712–70), the first half of which reads: "Two yellow warblers sing in the azure willow; / a file of white herons ascends the blue sky." Of the four of Bashō's hokku at the end, the first hypermetric one (twenty-one syllables) does not seem to allude to any particular Chinese source, but has an unmistakable Chinese flavor in its phrasing and imagery. The second hokku is a parody as it refers to a brief description of a temple called Rich Mountain that appears in an old Chinese text, *The Classic of Mountains and Seas:* "When frost falls, the bells at Rich Mountain ring." The third hokku is based on a well-known observation in *Chuang Tzu*: "When the mole drinks at the river, he takes no more than a bellyful." The last hokku is not particularly Chinese in tone or allusion, but is, like the other three, a reflection on his isolated state; the condensed phrase, "with rice cakes my echoes," means that the festive sounds of pounding steamed rice to make cakes for the New Year are remote to the poet's eremitic existence. Discernible in these and other pieces of this period is a man no longer content to be verbally clever and playful.

Toward the end of 1682 a great fire struck Edo and Bashō's house was one of the thousands that burnt down. For the better part of the following year he had a hard time, until his patrons and students put up money and rebuilt his house. The distinctive feature of Bashō's haikai that emerged then—in place of a deliberate sense of self-mockery and angst—was a positive delight in unconventional behavior. The hokku he used to open his account of a journey he began in the eighth month of 1684, later to be known as *Nozarashi Kikō* (Skull-Exposed-in-a-Field Diary), shows the new phase well:

Nozarashi o kokoro ni kaze no shimu mi kana
Skull exposed in a field in my mind—the wind pierces my body

The sentiment of this hokku appears serious and pessimistic, until one notes that no one sets out on a journey thinking of dying and turning into a skeleton. In describing himself in such an exaggerated manner Bashō is, in a way, showing off. This posturing is most pronounced in his hokku in the first of several renga he composed with people in Nagoya. The heading and first four parts of the sequence read:

Hat tattered by the rains during this long journey, and paper garment rumpled by the storms in each place, here is a solitary man who has known solitude—even I feel pity for him. As it occurs to me that once a man talented in mad tanka reached this province, may I say the following:

Mad hokku: in a tree-searing wind do I resemble Chikusai!

Bashō

who's that? off his hat a sasanqua has bounced   Yasui

at dawn moon the water-steward playing a bar owner   Kakei

the red horse shakes the dew off his head   Jūgo

Chikusai, the man referred to in the heading and hokku, is a fictitious quack who traveled about, spewing "mad" or humorous tanka. Bashō introduces this figure less for self-deprecation than for projecting himself as a man of *fūkyō* or *fūryū,* transcendental or poetic eccentricity. Cherishing such eccentricity is originally Taoist, and *Chuang Tzu,* a book that was frequently cited at the time to explain haikai, depicts men of spiritual attainment essentially as great eccentrics. For example: "the sage does not work at anything, does not pursue profit, does not dodge harm, does not enjoy being sought after, does not follow the Way, says nothing yet says something, says something yet says nothing, and wanders beyond the dust and grime. . . . The sage leans on the sun and moon, tucks the universe under his arm, merges himself with things, leaves the confusion and muddle as it is, and looks on slaves as exalted. Ordinary men strain and struggle; the sage is stupid and blockish." Or, as "Big Concealment," who is thought to represent the Taoist sage in the same book, observes, "Aimless wandering does not know what it seeks; demented drifting does not know where it goes. A wanderer, idle, unbound, I view the sights of Undeception. What more do I know?"

This Taoist-inspired attitude did not, in its overt form, stay long with Bashō; but, as an underlying motif it remained an important element of haikai throughout his career, and it has remained so to this day. He himself explained variations of this conceit on different occasions. For instance, Kyorai discusses some of the observations made on his hokku:

Iwa-hana ya koko ni mo hitori tsuki no kyaku
Nose of a boulder—here, too, is another guest of the moon

When Kyorai told Bashō of someone's suggestion that the last five should be *tsuki no saru*, "another monkey under the moon," Bashō asked him how he came to write the hokku. Told that he did it as he happened upon a poet while admiring the moon and strolling, Bashō said, "Only if you mean to introduce yourself by 'here, too, is another guest of the moon,' will the piece suggest some *fūryū*." He probably meant that such obtrusiveness or imposition, a behavior normally condemned, was thought admirable in a poet.

In a renga sequence Bashō wrote with Shita Yaba (1663–1740) in the year of his death occurs the following linking:

24   high above the paulownia tree the moon is clear   Yaba

25 "I closed the gate and went to bed, wordless, for the fun
      of it"   Bashō

According to Hattori Tohō (1657–1730), Bashō considered his line here the focal point in the *Sumidawara* (Charcoal Bag), the anthology that includes the renga. The *fūryū* of the person Bashō describes lies in his contrary decision not to stay up and admire the moon.

The following hokku by Yosa Buson (1716–83) may be cited as yet another example:

Negi kōte kareki no naka o kaerikeri
I buy scallions and go home through leafless trees

Buson, who was an accomplished painter as well and is often called an impressionist among haikai poets, is not projecting the contrast between the green of the scallions and the gray of the winter woods. Rather, he is saying that he, or whoever the speaker of the hokku is, has enough sense of *fūryū* to get out in the cold of the winter, buy lowly scallions, come home through a denuded forest, and still enjoy himself.

As noted, however, Bashō's obvious posturing as an eccentric receded after a while. Indeed, during the same journey the so-called Shōfū, or Bashō style, began to emerge, so that the *Fuyu no Hi* (Winter Day), the anthology consisting of the five sequences he wrote with the people in Nagoya, became the first of what were later to be set apart as "Bashō's Seven Anthologies." Shōfū may be defined as an attempt to describe reality perceptively and without forced sentiment. The sequence that opens with "mad hokku," though the first in the *Fuyu no Hi,* has, for example, this link by Bashō:

10   by the unfaded tablet, crying, disheartened   Kakei

11   a shadow, daybreak cold, making a fire   Bashō

Kakei's line, following an image suggested by the preceding part, describes a mother whose baby died. Following it, Bashō gives an ambiguous, yet strong picture. The third sequence in the same anthology has the following:

18   milk-vetches and violets in a field of six acres   Tokoku

19   happily warbling skylarks titi-ing titi-ing   Bashō

And the last sequence opens:

1   *Shimotsuki ya kō no tsukutsuku narabiite*   Kakei
   Frost Month: storks standing about absently

2   *fuyu no asahi no aware narikeri*   Bashō
   the winter morning sun is truly affecting

Of his waki to Kakei's hokku, Bashō later explained that its haikai lay in the way he responded, making the pair read like a tanka. But from the viewpoint of Shōfū, its virtue lies in its unassuming simplicity. Kakei's hokku is unusual: against the traditional prescription, it does not end, with the Japanese equivalent of a present participle without the rest of the verb formation. Several months afterward Bashō himself wrote a hokku of a similar construction:

Karasaki no matsu wa hana yori oboro nite
The pines of Karasaki, more blurred than the blossoms

Like Kakei's hokku, this one, in the original, gives an unfinished feeling as if the sentence was cut prematurely in the middle. When some people questioned this apparent solecism in hokku construction and his students defended it, Bashō simply said that was the way he perceived the landscape he described.

During the same period Bashō wrote other hokku that exemplify his new approach. One morning in the tenth month, in Kuwana, he wrote the following:

Yuki usushi shirauo shiroki koto issun
Snow thin: a white fish is white, just an inch

Soon he revised the first five to read *akebono ya,* "daybreak," saying he "deeply regretted" the original version, presumably because the combination of snow and white fish was too much. Then, on the nineteenth of the twelfth month, at Atsuta:

Umi kurete kamo no koe honokani shiroshi
The sea darkens, and the voices of ducks faintly white

This previously quoted synesthetic piece began a completed *kasen* of thirty-six parts, with Hayashi Tōyō (died 1712), who was the host, writing the waki:

> *kushi ni kujira o aburu sakazuki*
> whale broiled on skewers, and this cup

In the following year, 1685, he offered the following hokku for a a kasen session at Atsuta:

Nani to wa nashi ni nani yara yukashi sumire-gusa
I cannot say how, but elegant somehow, violets

Someone identified as Kōtan wrote the waki:

> *amigasa shikite kawazu kiki oru*
> sitting on his braided hat he listens to the frogs

As he returned to Edo, Bashō changed the hypermetric first seven syllables of his hokku to read *yamaji kite* (regular five syllables), "coming by a mountain path." The change made the image more clear, and the hokku has been known since then by the revised version.

All this can be said to have prepared Bashō to write the next year the most famous hokku of his and of all hokku:

Furuike ya kawazu tobikomu mizu no oto
An old pond: a frog jumps in—the sound of water

As may be expected, this hokku has some elements that make it haikai in the traditional sense. It echoes, among others, the following anonymous tanka in the *Kokinshū* (no. 125):

Kawazu naku Ide no yamabuki chirinikeri
hana no sakari ni awamashi mono o

The kerria roses at Ide where frogs croak have scattered;
I wish I had seen those blossoms at their prime!

This, as well as the observation in the preface to the anthology that "the voice of the frogs that live in the water" is one of the things that stir poetic thoughts, set the rule that required the poet, in mentioning the frog, to bring in kerria roses for the background and exclusively to refer to the amphibian's croaks. As Tohō pointed out, the haikai of this hokku is Bashō's departure from this tradition—namely, his decision to describe the "echo of a frog getting out of a wild grass bush" into the water. But as Tohō went on to observe, in a larger sense, *haikai no makoto,* or "the essence of haikai," was by Tohō's time felt to lie in the poet's unadorned description of whatever struck him as worthy of his response. It is in this larger sense that this hokku has been regarded as a landmark in Shōfū.

Of course, in the world of renga, constrained by tradition, rules, and the diverse temperaments of its participants, Bashō could not radically redirect what was being done, even if he wanted to. In many of the pieces written after the 1684–86 period he frequently returned to traditional, if not old-fashioned, approaches and ideals. Also, beside the treatises on his poetics written by his students (which are all thought to cover his opinions in the last several years of his life), his first known words on the subject did not appear until late 1689, when in the course of a kasen session he advised the participants not to be "heavy." (See *A Farewell Gift to Sora*, pages 93–106). In the meantime, as a professional poet he fine-tuned his techniques and, as a man who is said to have "grown thin" in his constant struggle to attain a "new fragrance," he changed his style, some have argued, seven times between the *Fuyu no Hi* and his death. But the approach that crystallized in his description of an old pond and a frog jumping in it remained the backbone of his poetics for the rest of his life.

What follows is a selection of Bashō's links written from 1687 to 1694, the year he died. The selection, arranged in rough chronological order, has been made to reflect two of his statements: "Someone who doesn't even know the Tōkaidō Road [the nation's artery, connecting Edo and Kyoto] shouldn't be confident in haikai," and "Haikai ought to be written by a child three feet tall." Though contradictory, these statements together epitomize the spirit of Shōfū.

in the lantern a giant candle smoulders high   Kyorai

    the flood pushes valley lumber downstream   Bashō

～

    for my small desolate field I'll make a scarecrow   Shifū

the horse at my grass hut, seized for my sakè debt   Bashō

～

    Asakusa rice goes out of the estuary   Jūshin

chins along the railing in the evening cool   Bashō

～

reaping the wheat that grew naturally in an old field   Tōyō

    someone's calling—must be corralling the horses   Bashō

~

    he leaves with watermelons on his horse   Kasshin

in this cold autumn, paid in pints of rice   Bashō

~

a bonze visits—how sad!—a grave in the field   Ichiryū

    chased, a deer runs off, abandoning its fawn   Bashō

~

the lawsuit drags on that blocks the reaping of autumn paddies
    Etsujin

    again and again he comes to ask how to write   Bashō

~

    in the storm, clouds spit the moon out   Yūgiku

on the autumn mountain the voice of a praying wild exorcist
    Bashō

~

at dawn they make a bonfire on their raft   Kisen

    a blue willow caressing their ruddy heads   Bashō

~

with a cup lying nearby, hugging the foot-warmer   Sora

    an old man alone serves out the day   Bashō

~

a sled for firewood has left this long trail   Sora

    each warrior's holing up for winter in his house   Bashō

~

still young enough to care for dolls, and beautiful   Sukan

    the koto she holds must be heavy on her lap   Bashō

~

ELEGANCE, HUMOR, AND POETRY · *83*

though the northern star doesn't move, the clouds block it

                Seifū

 today too for Zen meditation he climbs the rock   Bashō

           ~

field mice have ravaged the rice under the clear moon Hanzan

 the wind grows chilly as he travels with calves   Bashō

           ~

 from a tenuous point her love has grown intense Kyokusui

when lost in thought, she's prodded to eat   Bashō

           ~

rustling, rustling, he makes sandals as the moon shines Bonchō

 she got up to shake off the fleas—it's early fall   Bashō

         ~

for my evening meal I eat sand eels, and the wind's fragrant

                Bonchō

 scratching a leech bite-mark and feeling good   Bashō

         ~

daybreak moon in the blue sky, as the morning comes Kyorai

 autumn over the lake water, first frost on Hira   Bashō

         ~

at parting she warms his kimono that became cold Sensen

 both being young, their love is innocent   Bashō

         ~

past midnight when the pine wind blows, gust after gust Shikō

 the gate keeper announces that there's a foundling Bashō

         ~

 to make the bridegroom feel at home, they frequent the
 pawnshop

                Shadō

setting aside the best part for him at mealtime   Bashō

         ~

even eggplants and cowpeas know what they are   Roten

a hawk chick crumples its claws at a skylark   Bashō

~

on the ferry boat I ask the name of a grass   Ii

a gallinules' nest has a pile of red heads   Bashō

~

even while slicing dried vegetables for topping rice, she's absent-minded   Yaba

the days he doesn't take his horse out, they make love inside   Bashō

~

outside the town, vacant shops mostly locked   Baken

carrying a samisen, a traveling beggar   Bashō

~

sound of winds thunderously hitting the nettle-tree   Yaba

he unties the rope from the rice thief   Bashō

~

(hokku)

The snow scatters and reaches the hood under his hat   Sampū

over his sword hilt, a frozen towel   Bashō

~

today too they plot how to have fun   Taisui

their parents were popular—these young doctors   Bashō

~

the path buried under bamboo grass—fascinating!   Tempo

"Watch your head," says the note on the gate   Bashō

~

simply over the mid-plain the moon is clear   Santen

thunder remains tongue-tied, giving no news   Bashō

~

ELEGANCE, HUMOR, AND POETRY   ·   *85*

light snow has made a round of the entire yard　　　Shikō

　in the lord's presence, hushed, the next folk dance　　Bashō

~

saying he came to pay respect to the shrine, and forgiven for
　his theft　　　　　　　　　　　　　　　　　　Rōka

　with a grin, a layer of cloud welcomes the morning sun
　　　　　　　　　　　　　　　　　　　　　　　Bashō

~

the lady-in-waiting, returned to her village, is lachrymose
　　　　　　　　　　　　　　　　　　　　　　　Jōsō

　putting things out of the lacquered box, putting them in
　　　　　　　　　　　　　　　　　　　　　　　Bashō

~

visibly colder than the river, the birds' voices　　　Hōjin

　the rice of this village has no rice taste　　　　Bashō

~

in the moonlight the cloud color suggests snow　　　Shikō

　finished, palanquin bearers divide the money　　　Bashō

~

　she says foul things to the bride and her own daughter
　　　　　　　　　　　　　　　　　　　　　　　Shikō

all the guests are cold, freezing, in the room with a foot-
　warmer　　　　　　　　　　　　　　　　　　　Bashō

~

the drugstore owner doesn't seem terribly busy　　　Bōsui

　three years now, but his bride has no child　　　Bashō

~

now at long last the silver exchange deal is closed　Bōsui

　without fuss he downs the prescribed drug　　　Bashō

~

red cockscombs, right at the center of the garden   Inen

he's managed to calm down his daughter's unsettled heart
                                                    Bashō

~

he was supposed to send a messenger but somehow forgot
                                                    Shikō

he had switched his, but the doctor came to call   Bashō

~·~ CHAPTER THREE ~·~

Bashō and Poetry Writing as a Group Activity

• Renga at the Time of Bashō •

By Bashō's time, writing hokku independent of renga had be-
come pervasive. Of the slightly less than one thousand hokku
that Bashō is believed to have written, only one hundred thirty-
five began renga sequences. To put it differently, he was us-
ing a hokku for the original purpose of beginning a renga only
once every seven times. Still, the importance of renga for
Bashō and his determination to live by it are beyond question.
From the first known sequence with his participation in 1665,
till the last in 1694, he took part in three hundred seventy-
eight recorded sessions; in some he simply provided one
link, while in others he presided over a whole sequence.
This is an average of thirteen sessions a year. (The figure jumps
to thirty a year if only the last ten years of his life are con-
sidered.) The importance of renga for Bashō can also be seen
in several notable treatises on his poetics that were written by
his disciples. These devote the majority of their texts to the
technical discussions of renga, rather than hokku.

What was a renga session like in Bashō's time? The rules on
the conduct of a session developed early and became more
complex and rigid over the centuries. Although Bashō is known
to have been wary and often scornful of strict rules, in a typical
session the master (*sōshō*) and the scribe (*shūhitsu*) played the
leading roles. The master was responsible for controlling the

progress of the session by weighing the skills of various participants and for maintaining a good atmosphere, a certain degree of poetic quality, and everyone's interest in the proceedings. The scribe, who was chosen from the participants other than the master in most cases, had to be above all a good calligrapher with orthographic knowledge. But his role was far from mechanical. He pointed out the violations of rules, prodded the slow versifiers, and assigned key parts to appropriate persons. Because he tended to know the participants intimately, he was expected to do all this without ruffling anyone's feelings. He also recited the parts—the hokku five times in all, the others twice each. In practice sessions the scribe doubled as a master.

The room for a renga session usually had an alcove decorated with a scroll painting of Sugawara no Michizane, the patron deity of renga, or a scroll with the characters indicating him. In front of the alcove were a low desk and a round cushion, both intended for the scribe. The master usually sat to the scribe's right. Ideally, the room was to be in a larger setting, such as the one described by Yoshimoto: "When you think of holding a session, first choose the time and look for sweeping scenery. During the snow or the moonlight, or when flowering trees are about to end, if you look at the way they change with the passage of time, your heart will stir, and the words will come out. If choose you must, choose a place not only with sweeping scenery but also with a [good] landscape. Mulling over poetic thoughts by facing the mountains and viewing the waters, you will have the best results." Yoshimoto, an aristocrat, spoke for elegant, orthodox renga, but it is doubtful that such classical settings were readily available even to him, the highest ranking court official. They certainly were not to the plebeian Bashō. However, Bashō, like Sōgi, sought such settings by traveling, and different though his brand of renga was from Yoshimoto's, he tried to incorporate in hokku this larger perception of nature.

The person responsible for the overall operation of a renga meeting was either its sponsor or the caretaker of the group that wanted it. He picked the participants, selected the place, and played the host. He paid the master and, when the latter was traveling, provided him with lodgings and other accommodations. Most often the master, being the guest of honor, wrote the hokku, while the host wrote the wakiku. As we have seen, the arrangement of having the guest make a complimentary statement in the hokku and the host respond in kind in the wakiku existed from the outset. But the salutatory nature of the opening exchange was often of crucial importance to masters like Bashō, who earned their living from such sessions. Bashō's attitude toward this is vividly described in a story told by Kyorai. Once, the two men participated in a renga session hosted by another member of Bashō's school, Mizuta Masahide (1657–1723). After it was over and they reached the house where they were to stay that night, Bashō harshly reprimanded Kyorai: "Tonight you met at Masahide's house for the first time. Because you were the most welcome guest, you should have expected in advance that the hokku was to be yours. Moreover, when asked for the hokku, you should have promptly come up with one, forgetting about whether it was good or bad. How much time do we have in one night? If you had spent too much time on your hokku, the meeting this evening might have been ruined. That was utterly tasteless of you. It was so disheartening that I did the hokku. At once Masahide added the wakiku. His was a fierce description of the sky, but the daisan you followed it with was so slack. All that was regrettable."

For Bashō, Kyorai's sin was threefold. First, he failed to anticipate his position as guest of honor and prepare a hokku or two for the occasion. Second, even though that failure itself might have been overlooked, he compounded it by failing to respond readily when told what was expected of him. His lack of alacrity and tact was probably the result of his honest attempt to write a respectable hokku; but it was embarrassing to his host, as well as to Bashō, his teacher. Finally, when Bashō stood in for him and Masahide responded with the promptness expected of a host, Kyorai failed to catch the taut spirit of the host's wakiku. As Kyorai says at the beginning of his account, Bashō drastically rewrote his piece.

Some of Bashō's renga during his journey to the north in 1689 well illustrate the salutatory nature of the opening part. (Bashō later described the journey in his celebrated travel diary *Oku no Hosomichi* [The Narrow Road to the Interior].) He undertook the journey partly to expand his turf, so to speak, as a renga poet; and while renewing some acquaintanceships, he met many new people. His first important renga host was Kanokobata Suitō, a young samurai of twenty-seven he had known from Edo. The greetings between them went like this:

Magusa ou hito o shiori no natsuno kana   Bashō
Someone carrying hay my marker through this summer field

   aoki ichigo o kobosu shii no ha   Suitō
   green strawberries sprinkled on pasania leaves

This is a classical exchange. Though a man of considerable means, Suitō's house was in the middle of wild fields. Seizing on the notion, originally Chinese, that a true man of refinement lives a rustic life, Bashō compliments his host by saying that he found his residence only by following a peasant who appeared to know the area well. In response, Suitō deprecates himself: "All I could come up with to welcome you is unripe strawberries on the few leaves I managed to find in my garden." This is just a manner of speaking, to put it mildly; as the *Oku no Hosomichi* makes clear, Suitō entertained Bashō well for the two weeks he stayed with him. "Summer" and "strawberries" are mentioned because the fourth month when this session was held is the beginning of summer by the lunar calendar. This renga was a kasen, with seven participants.

The second host worth mentioning is Sagara Tōkyū (1638–1715), and his first exchange with Bashō reads:

Fūryū no hajime ya Oku no taue-uta   Bashō
Beginning of poetry: this rice-planting song of the Interior

ichigo o otte waga mōke gusa   Tōkyū
strawberries laid on the grass, I've waited

Bashō again praises his host. Only a few days earlier he had
passed through the Shirakawa Barrier, the gateway to the In-
terior. Said to have been built in the fifth century as the north-
ernmost fort to fend off the Ainu, the barrier had probably
ceased to exist by the tenth century. But precisely because of
that legendary existence, it became one of the places any self-
respecting poet had to mention in his poetry. Bashō's compli-
ments are implied in his admiration for the host for living
near such a poetic spot ("beginning of poetry") and in finding
himself with him at the propitious rice-planting time that had
just begun. Tōkyū responds by pointing out that he is too
humble to deserve such words of praise, but that nonetheless
he is pleased to meet him. The coincidence of a young host and
then a middle-aged one mentioning strawberries may have
amused Bashō. This kasen was written by Bashō, Tōkyū, and
Bashō's companion for the journey, Kaai Sora (1649–1710). In
the *Oku no Hosomichi* Bashō says the three of them did two more
sequences, but only the first three parts of each of the other two
remain.

Toward the end of the fifth month, Bashō and Sora stayed at
the "river official" Takano Ichi'ei's house that overlooked the
Mogami River, renowned for its swift currents. The thirty-six-
part sequence they did during their time together (with partic-
ipation of a fourth person) naturally began with Bashō praising
the host and the host deprecating himself:

Samidare o atsumete suzushi Mogami-gawa   Bashō
Gathering the May rains, and cool, the Mogami River

kishi ni hotaru o tsunagu funagui   Ichi'ei
the pole for boats moors fireflies to the bank

It is at the peak of the rainy season, and Bashō compliments
Ichi'ei on the fullness of the river, of which the host is in charge
if only locally, that makes the atmosphere feel cool. Ichi'ei

replies that he is just a humble pole for boats keeping the honorable guests ("fireflies") for a while. Bashō later changed *suzushi* (cool) to *hayashi* (swift) in order to make his hokku less salutatory but more effective as a poem.

If we assume the journey to the Interior ended where Bashō ends his account, in the early ninth month, it lasted just over five months. But he continued to visit places for two more years and did not return to Edo until the end of 1691. This five-month period was Bashō's most productive: he presided over poetry workshops, to use a modern term, thirty-six times, or once every four days. The intensity of his work on renga may partly account for the structure of the *Oku no Hosomichi,* which some say resembles that of the thirty-six-part sequence.

The journey also produced the only renga sequence retaining Bashō's revisions and comments. This *Sequence Revised by Bashō* (*Okina Naoshi no Maki*) is also known as *A Farewell Gift to Sora* (*Sora Sen*) because it was composed when Sora had to part company with Bashō due to an ailment that had been troubling him for some time. Sora's departure is accorded a passage in the *Oku no Hosomichi:*

> *Sora had stomach trouble, and because he had relatives in a place called Nagashima in the province of Ise, went ahead, leaving me with:*
>
> Iki-ikite taore fufu tomo hagi no hara   Sora
> Going on and on I might collapse—in a bush-clover field
>
> *The one going, saddened, the one left behind, despondent, we were like single ducks after parting, lost in clouds. I added:*
>
> Kyō yori ya kakitsuke kesan kasa no tsuyu
> From today on, erase the inscript, dew on my hat

Bashō's reference to "ducks" alludes to the poem the Chinese official Su Wu is said to have written to bid farewell to Li Ling when they parted after Su Wu was released from detention by the Hsiung-nu in 81 B.C. The poem begins:

Two wild ducks flew north together;
one alone now soars southward.
You must remain here in your lodge,
I must return to my old home.

The "inscript" in Bashō's hokku is the one pilgrims and other people used to make on the large hats they wore on long journeys. The wording of such an inscript usually went, "In heaven and earth, we two homeless companions," the two originally meaning the Lord Buddha and the traveler. If such was Bashō's inscript, by "two" he might have meant Sora and himself. "Dew," a kigo for autumn, is here used in its old metaphorical sense of tears as well.

A Farewell Gift to Sora was published two years later, in 1691, by Tachibana Hokushi (died 1718), the third participant in the thirty-six-part renga, although the version with Bashō's revisions and comments recorded by Hokushi was not published until 1839. Hokushi joined Bashō and Sora in Kanazawa in the middle of the seventh month, and by the time the three of them sat down in the early eighth month to write the sequence at a hot spring in Yamanaka, he had participated in five sessions with Bashō and others. In this respect, the sequence is unlike many others written during the journey in which Bashō hardly knew most of the participants.

A FAREWELL GIFT TO SORA

1 *Uma karite tsubame oiiku wakare kana*   Hokushi
  Renting a horse you follow the swallows as we part

  Category: Autumn.   Kigo: swallows. The ailing Sora rented a horse and headed south, the direction in which swallows were now returning. This hokku is salutatory in expressing the sadness of parting in an open, natural way. There is no comment by Bashō.

2   *hanano midaruru yama no magarime*   Sora
    fields of flowers disturbed where the mountain turns

Autumn. Kigo: fields of flowers. Sora returns the salutation. His original version was *hanano ni takaki iwa no magarime,* "fields of flowers where a tall boulder turns." Bashō made the change probably because Sora's phrasing was somewhat flat in sentiment and attracted too much attention to "a tall boulder." "Disturbed" is meant to reflect the departing person's state of mind.

3 *tsuki yoshi to sumō ni hakama fuminugite*　　　　Bashō
　　saying, "The moon's good," they kick off their *hakama* for
　　wrestling

Autumn. Kigo: moon. Bashō originally had *tsuki haruru,* "with the moon clear," for the first five syllables. He made the change to accommodate the change in the wakiku: to avoid a similar phrasing (*midaruru* and *haruru*) and to make the focus of the action sharper. *Hakama* are men's formal pantslike wear and suggest young samurai. A switch is skillfully made from day to night and from people bidding farewell to people preparing to wrestle.

4　*saya bashirishi o yagate tomekeri*　　　　Hokushi
　　sword running out of its scabbard stopped in a moment

Miscellaneous. Hokushi originally wrote *tomo no,* "by a friend," instead of *yagate* (in a moment). Bashō said it was "heavy." He is thought to have meant that the introduction of a definite human figure either cluttered the overall image or made the action too explanatory. (Several months later, in the fourth month of 1690, he wrote to Miyazaki Shikin [1673–1735] and his brother Sensen [died 1706] and urged them to "try not to be heavy-handed and roundabout in haikai and hokku." His emphasis on *karumi,* lightness, in his final years probably took shape during this period.) A sword, if tilted in the wrong way when not fastened with a ferrule, easily ran out of its scabbard and could be dangerous. The sword sliding out in that manner was also a metaphor for an impetuous, impudent man.

5 *aobuchi ni uso no tobikomu mizu no oto*　　　　Sora
　　into the blue depths an otter jumps—the sound of water

Miscellaneous. Bashō mulled over this and suggested changing the first five syllables to read *nisan biki,* "two or three [otters]." But after a while he said, "'Into the blue depths' is just fine," and went back to Sora's original. If Sora and Bashō felt anything about this verse in relation to Bashō's famous hokku, that is not known.

6   *shiba kari kokasu mine no sasamichi*   Bashō
    he fells brushwood along the hilltop bamboo grass path

Miscellaneous. In working this out, Bashō thought of using *tadoru,* "to follow," or *kayou,* "to frequent," instead of *kokasu* (fell). With the former word, the meaning becomes "a brushwood gatherer follows the hilltop bamboo grass path," and with the latter, "brushwood gatherers frequent the hilltop bamboo grass path." He decided against either, probably because neither has the immediacy of the original word.

7 *arare furu hidari no yama wa Suge no tera*   Hokushi
    "On that hail-falling mountain to the left is the Temple of Suge"

Winter. Kigo: hail. Hokushi's initial version had *matsu fukaki,* "pine-deep," for the first five syllables. Bashō changed it probably to carry forward the sense of movement indicated by *kokasu* (fell).

8   *yūjo shigo nin inaka watarai*   Sora
    four or five prostitutes making a round of the countryside

Miscellaneous. Sora had *yakusha,* "actors," instead of *yūjo* (prostitutes). Both are wretched people making a living traveling, but Bashō decided that prostitutes would evoke more pity in the cold weather suggested by "hail-falling."

9 *rakugaki ni koishiki kimi ga na mo arite*   Bashō
    "In these graffiti is the name of someone I love"

Love. Bashō initially had *koshibari ni* for the first five syllables; *koshibari* is the paper pasted on the lower part of a wall or a sliding door and suggests an inn where the prostitutes are staying. He changed it probably to make the effect less specific, less busy.

10   *kami wa soranedo uo kuwanu nari*   Hokushi
       he hasn't shaven his head but doesn't eat fish

Buddhism.   Bashō praised Hokushi for "grasping the heart" of the preceding part. Hokushi's description suggests someone who has decided to take Buddhist vows by becoming a vegetarian—Buddhism proscribes consumption of anything sentient —but whose resolve to enter priesthood is not firm enough to shave his head. This part's connection to the preceding one is that the person still has an attachment to love and other worldly matters.

11 *hasu no ito toru mo nakanaka tsumi fukaki*   Sora
     "Making thread from lotus is itself a sinful thing"

Buddhism.   Bashō also praised Sora for this one. Making thread out of lotus pod fiber refers to the legend of Princess Chūjō, who is said to have woven a mandala out of such thread. Sora's part says that making thread out of the lotus, a plant sacred for Buddhists, is a pious act, but that when viewed from the absolutist, Buddhist proscriptions it too is a sinful thing.

12   *senzo no hin o tsutaetaru mon*   Bashō
       ancestral poverty lives on at this mansion

Miscellaneous.   Bashō first had *shigo dai,* "four or five generations," instead of *senzo no* (ancestral). One reason for the change is obvious: the phrase, "four or five," is used in the eighth part. Another reason may be that "ancestral" is larger in concept, strengthening the irony of the observation. The relation of this part to the preceding one is that someone who regards as sinful the pious act of making thread out of lotus pods is likely to be at best an eccentric who, probably because of his considerable pedigree, flaunts the family tradition of destitution.

13 *ariake no matsuri no jōza katakunashi*   Hokushi
   under the daybreak moon the ceremony's high chair is
   obstinate

Autumn. Kigo: daybreak moon. This part requires that the
moon be mentioned. Hokushi first had *yoitsuki ni,* "under the
evening moon," for the first five syllables. This cryptic part
may mean that the man given the honor of supervising a
traditional ceremony is stubborn. Bashō made the change
probably because daybreak, suggesting a prolonged all-night
ceremony, is more appropriate for such a person and occasion.

14   *tsuyu mazu harau kari no yumi-take*   Sora
   dew first brushed aside for bamboo to make a hunting
   bow

Autumn. Kigo: dew. Linked to the thirteenth part, this
suggests someone who is, early in the morning, looking for fine
bamboo with which to make a ceremonial hunting bow. But
the linking factor is tenuous, with only the similar feelings ex-
pressed making the connection possible. Tenuousness in linking
was not altogether discouraged, but sometimes considered neces-
sary.

15 *akikaze wa mono iwanu ko mo namida nite*   Bashō
   in the autumn wind even the silent child is in tears

Autumn. Kigo: autumn wind. Hokushi reports that when
he told Bashō this part was excellent, Bashō returned the
compliment, saying both he and Sora wrote parts equally good.
With the introduction of a child who doesn't say anything, the
preceding part is made to suggest a poor hunter or a masterless
samurai.

16   *shiroki tamoto no tsuzuku sōrei*   Hokushi
   white sleeves continue at this funeral rite

Miscellaneous.   A different reason is given for the child's
tears. In those days white was the color for funerals.

17 *hana no ka wa furuki miyako no machi zukuri*   Sora
   fragrance of flowers and town construction in the ancient
   capital

Spring. Kigo: flowers. Sora had *hana no ka ni Nara no miyako
no machi zukuri,* "in the fragrance of flowers, town construction
in the capital of Nara." Bashō's revision was probably intended
to make the description less specific and more suggestive. This
part requires a mention of cherry flowers. Sora, with or without
Bashō's revision, is thought to have met that requirement very
well, when it was awkward to do so after a description of a
funeral.

18   *haru o nokoseru Genjō no hako*   Bashō
     Genjō's box retains spring

Spring. Kigo: spring. Genjō, the first son of Satomura
Jōha, wrote orthodox renga. The Satomura family was from
Nara and was by then providing the shogunate with official renga
instructors. Genjō himself died quite young. By "Genjo's
box" Bashō probably intended to suggest a traditional poetic
atmosphere.

19 *nodokasa ya Shirara Naniwa no kai-zukushi*   Hokushi
   serenity: all the seashells of Shirara, Naniwa

Spring. Kigo: serenity (*nodokasa*). Hokushi initially had
kai ōshi, "many seashells," for the last five syllables. Bashō's
change shifts the focus from the two beaches mentioned to the
box in the preceding part, for listing *all* of one category (*zukushi*)
was common in books, illustrations, paintings. Here, "all the
seashells" could be a reference to the design on Genjō's box,
which is most likely to be lacquered.

20   *gin no konabe ni idasu seri-yaki*   Sora
     in a small silver pot he serves broiled parsley

Spring or Winter. Kigo: broiled parsley. This is a delight
for annotators. The preceding part suggests what may be de-

scribed as a world of "un-urbane elegance" because of the reference to seashells. In response, Sora introduces a "small silver pot," indicating a person of refined taste with a certain tilt in his attitude. He then fulfills the expectation by mentioning "broiled parsley," a recipe thought to be especially *sabi*—the quality of being elegant in deprivation. Parsley was actually cooked in a pot, but here it is described as "broiled," giving a poetic touch to the recipe. (Sora apparently left soon after writing this part, for this is the last time he appears in the sequence.)

Bashō then thought up two possible links and, deciding that the beginning phrase of both, *temakura ni*, "arm for a pillow," would be a good connecting image, urged Hokushi to try himself. By Bashō:

temakura ni omou koto naki mi narikeri
arm for a pillow, he's someone with nothing to worry about

temakura ni noki no tama-mizu nagame wabi
arm for a pillow, watching the gemlike raindrops from the
    eaves, alone

Hokushi came up with two:

temakura no yodare tsutōte mezamekeru
arm for a pillow, drool dribbling, and waking

temakura ni take fuki wataru yūmagure
arm for a pillow: a wind blows through bamboos in the
    evening dark

Finally, Bashō decided to use the following, another of his own:

21 *temakura ni shitone no hokori uchi-harai*   Bashō
    arm for a pillow, he brushes dust off his princely bed

Miscellaneous. Bashō rejected the four possibilities because they all had some problems. His first is too abstract. His second contains some technical problems. If "broiled parsley" were taken to represent the category of spring, this would continue the same theme for five consecutive parts, or too long. If, on the other hand, "broiled parsley" were to belong to the category of winter, that would mean dropping the theme of spring after three consecutive parts and returning to it only after one link on a different season, which is awkward. Hokushi's first possibility suggests a low-class servant, making its connection to the preceding part difficult; and his second, though not bad, is not quite right, suggesting a lonely court lady because of tanka using the same image. The version Bashō decided to use, in contrast, suggests a man of Proustian languor, thereby putting the man of the preceding part in sharper focus.

22 *utsukushikare to nozoku fukumen*   Hokushi
   hoping for a beauty he peers into the mask

Love. This suggests a prostitute summoned by the languid man of the preceding link. Women often wore masks when they went out.

23 *tsugi-kosode takimono-uri no kofū nari*   Bashō
   in a patchwork kimono he's an incense vender of the old style

Love. *Tsugi-kosode,* here translated "patchwork kimono," are comparable to quilts; they started out as utilitarian objects, but went on to become fashionable items. By Bashō's time they had become something that reminded one of the good old days. The "incense vender" here is a male prostitute in disguise. After several more parts were written, Bashō came back to this part, and said that *kosode* here and *shitone* in the twenty-first part sounded too much alike to be so close to each other, but that he couldn't come up with any solution.

24 *hikuraudo naru hito no kiku-hata*   Bashō
   once a junior chamberlain, now in his chrysanthemum garden

Autumn. Kigo: chrysanthemum. As is often the case when two persons write a sequence, Bashō writes two consecutive parts from now on; and so does Hokushi. A *hikuraudo,* here translated "junior chamberlain," worked at the court as an apprentice to a chamberlain. Usually a son of a good family, he was allowed to enter the court's inner quarters but his low rank was fixed. Bashō's description suggests such a junior chamberlain now retired and cultivating chrysanthemums for pleasure. With this, the "incense vender" in the preceding part becomes a true incense vender trying to sell his wares to a man of leisure.

25 *shigi futatsu dai ni nosete mo sabishisa yo* Hokushi
  even two snipes offered on a tray, wanting

Autumn. Kigo: snipes. The offering can be either to the retired junior chamberlain, or from him. Either way, the suggestion is that a normally respectable gift looks shabby in someone with an aristocratic air. Bashō praised Hokushi for his transition.

26 *aware ni tsukuru mikazuki no waki* Hokushi
  movingly he makes a waki on the crescent moon

Autumn. Kigo: crescent moon. Hokushi was reminded by the preceding part of a renga session, which usually had dining as part of its proceedings. (One notice for "haikai sessions" that Bashō is said to have had on his wall said, among other things, "Be content with whatever cheap food and cheap tea you may have" and "Don't get drunk and rowdy.") Hokushi notes that Bashō said, "There could also be a link like this," but what that comment meant is not clear.

27 *sho-hosshin kusa no makura ni tabine shite* Bashō
  a brand-new priest sleeping on a grass pillow, traveling

Buddhism. Bashō, after writing this, said, "This sort of link may be found in any sequence." He meant he didn't think it very good. The redundant combination of *kusa no makura* (grass pillow), an old metaphor for going to sleep while traveling, and *tabine*, which says exactly what the metaphor means, does make this a *yariku*, an easy or quick part chiefly meant to keep it going. When connected to the preceding part, it suggests a priest who has put up at an inn and joined a renga session.

28 *Obata mo chikashi Ise no kamikaze*   Bashō
    Obata is close by, and Ise's divine wind

Shintoism. Obata is an area just across a river from the Grand Shrine of Ise. Coupled with the preceding part, this one suggests a man who has traveled to pay homage to the shrine and, now finding himself close to it, is touched by a waft of wind from that direction. The "divine wind" refers to stories in the *Kojiki* and *Man'yōshū* that tell of the special wind from the Grand Shrine that helps those on the side of justice.

29 *hōsō wa Kuwana Hinaga mo hayari sugi*   Hokushi
    "The smallpox has already peaked in Kuwana, Hinaga"

Miscellaneous. Both Kuwana and Hinaga are near Ise. The suggestion is that the raging smallpox couldn't come too close to the Grand Shrine. Bashō praised Hokushi for his adroitness in employing the yotsude technique that brings up two items in response to two items in the preceding part—here, two place names set against two place names.

30 *ame hare kumoru biwa tsuwaru nari*   Hokushi
    "Rain, sun, or cloud, the loquats mellow"

Summer. Kigo: loquats. Hokushi originally had *hito ame goto ni*, "with each rainfall," for the first seven syllables. The connection of this part to the preceding one is the changeable weather when smallpox tended to occur.

31 *hosonagaki sennyo no sugata taoyaka ni*   Bashō
    the slender figure of a goddess, full of grace

Miscellaneous. Hokushi says Bashō smiled contentedly when praised for the excellence of this part. Nevertheless, and even though "loquats" and a lissom "goddess" strongly suggest an allusion to Chinese literature, the linking of this part to the preceding one is thought to be unclear.

32   *akane o shiboru mizu no shiranami*   Bashō
     wringing the madder, the water, the white waves

Miscellaneous. Standing alone, this suggests a woman washing madder-dyed cloths in the river, a common sight in those days. But when coupled with the preceding part, it turns a mortal female into a goddess. To use one annotator's image, Bashō painted an Utamaro picture of a Chinese goddess.

33 *Nakatsuna ga Uji no ajiro to uchi-nagame*   Hokushi
   Nakatsuna viewing it all as the weir of Uji

Winter.   Kigo: weir. Nakatsuna of the Minamoto clan was one of the generals who participated in the battle at the Uji River in 1180, the first important confrontation between the rebelling Minamoto clan and the ruling Taira clan. According to *The Tale of the Heike,* at one point during the battle a Taira general plunged all of his twenty-eight thousand warriors—a slight poetic exaggeration here—into the river, causing a great confusion. Among the many warriors pushed downstream by the strong currents, three in bright red armor got caught in the fishing weir. Mindful that the fishing weirs of the Uji River were a favorite topic of court poets, Nakatsuna, when he saw the men, composed a tanka:

> *Ise musha wa mina hiodoshi no yoroi kite*
> *Uji no ajiro ni kakarinuru kana*

> Ise warriors, all clad in fire-frightening armor,
> have been caught up in the weir of Uji!

Hokushi, in alluding to this episode in his part, gave a slight twist, lumping the warriors with the fishing gear. Bashō said, "This is another decoration in the sequence." He probably meant that the link was attractive, even though he no longer looked on this type of fancy turn favorably.

34   *tera ni tsukai o tateru kōjō*   Hokushi
      word for which a courier's dispatched to a temple

Miscellaneous. Hokushi, following his own description, came up with an easy response. For one thing, Uji has some well-known temples, so associating Uji with temples is logical. For another, because the leaders of Buddhist temples were heavily involved in the feud between the Minamoto and Taira clans, it is equally logical to imagine that a messenger or two were dispatched to temples to notify them of the consequences of such an important battle.

35 *kane tsuite asoban hana no chirikakaru*   Bashō
   I'll ring the bell for fun—flowers scatter on me

Spring. Kigo: flowers. When he came up with this part— the penultimate position that requires a mention of flowers— Bashō said he also thought of saying *chiraba chire* for the last five syllables but decided against it because it wasn't poetic enough. With *chiraba chire,* the line would mean: "I'll ring the bell for fun—flowers, scatter, if scatter you must!" Either way, the part recalls a famous tanka by Monk Nōin (born 988) in the *Shin Kokinshū* (no. 166):

Yamazato no haru no yūgure kite mireba
iriai no kane ni hana zo chirikeru

Coming to a mountain village in the spring evening,
at the bell at sundown, flowers scatter

The connection of this part to the preceding one is rather thin, except the association of a temple with a bell. One possibility is that the mock-serious tone of the thirty-fourth part prompted Bashō to think of a poetically minded person.

36 *suikyōnin to Yayoi kureyuku*   Bashō
    a zany and a March day in the growing dark

Spring. Kigo: March (*Yayoi*). As he wrote this, the ageku,
Bashō said to Hokushi that he simply described the person in
the preceding line. Such a zany or an eccentric, as we have
seen, is a favorite topic of haikai poetry. He added, "But be
careful with an ageku." He probably meant that despite the
tone in which he ended this sequence, one shouldn't often be
as lighthearted at the ending where a congratulatory tone is
the norm.

• Renga Since the Time of Bashō •

Bashō's comments preserved for *A Farewell Gift to Sora*, though
sketchy, show him as an astute, considerate, and flexible teacher
of poetry. Most striking is the fact that he often rewrote his
own compositions and openly brought up alternatives. He was
concerned more about poetry than about his appearance as a
"master" of the art. This attitude was behind his famous em-
phasis on constant change in style and approach. Using an
image he apparently liked, Bashō once warned those who
composed renga with him never to "lick the drool of a prede-
cessor," and added: "Just as the four seasons push and move
forward, things renew themselves. Everything is like that."
It was an admirable proposition, and in stating it Bashō was
doing what Yoshimoto had done three hundred years earlier.
But the essential nature of renga writing as a group activity,
the indigenous Japanese tendency to form teacher-student
relations, and resultant professionalization worked against
Bashō's ideal, as they had against Yoshimoto's. The popularity
of renga was maintained or even increased, but the quality
suffered.

To look at Yoshimoto's kind of orthodox renga first, it had
lost its literary value by the time Bashō began writing. But it

continued to hold an official place in the Tokugawa shogunate. The most honorable day in the year for the family with the hereditary right to provide instructors was the day in the first month when a sequence was composed with the shogun participating. Renga composition at that annual ceremony was highly stylized. At the crack of dawn the grand *sōshō* (or the poet laureate of sorts) put on his formal attire and led a troop of ten or more professional renga poets (who in time also acquired hereditary rights) to the Renga Room of Edo Castle. At about seven composition began. The shogun's participation was nominal at best. He did not even enter the room where the renga poets were sitting, staying instead in an adjacent room, and the wakiku, which he was supposed to compose, was actually written by the second-ranking *sōshō,* who submitted two possibilities beforehand for the shogun to pick. After hearing the recitation of the daisan, the shogun withdrew. The composition became equally nominal. At first the poets simply practiced in advance, but soon they began preparing the entire sequence well before the ritualistic gathering. Then the sequence, originally the standard length of one hundred parts, was shortened to that of forty-four parts, acronymically called *yoyoshi,* "the world is good." Under such circumstances any surviving motivation for change was lost. Formality was all that counted, and such formality could last only as long as it had institutional support. When a new government in the second half of the nineteenth century withdrew support, orthodox renga collapsed. The same thing happened to renga composed under the sponsorship of daimyo and at the imperial court, although Yamada Yoshio (1873–1958), whose father was the instructor for a daimyo, continued to write and teach throughout his life, thereby considerably influencing some modern scholars of renga.

Haikai no renga went through a different decline. Because it was less ritualistic and had a greater appeal to common people, it became increasingly popular. By the early decades of the nineteenth century, the smallest gathering of people, as at a barbershop, is said to have prompted renga composition. Concurrently more people vied to get *sōshō* positions, and did. (As late as 1882, one survey counted twenty *sōshō*.) More professionalization and more codification ensued; that meant less poetry. Professionalization here, however, resulted in at least one good thing; to justify their profession *sōshō* deified Bashō and scholarship on his poetic achievements improved.

The popularity of haikai was accompanied, as in the preceding centuries, by the popularity of tsukeai or maeku-zuke: composing a link to a proposed part. During the eighteenth century, this led to the shortening of the minimum combination of two parts to a single part consisting of 5-7-5 syllables. The independence of the 5-7-5–syllable form had happened long before with hokku, but the 5-7-5–syllable form that grew out of maeku-zuke was considered separately from the hokku because it was free from kigo and other requirements imposed on the latter. The new genre came to be known as *senryū* in recognition of Karai Senryū (1718–90), who took the final step in abandoning maeku and published enormously popular collections of independent tsukeku. The difference between the tsukeku that were now thought dissociable from maeku and those that were previously printed with maeku can be seen in the following examples. Among the tsukeai that I have cited earlier from the *Inu Tsukubashū*, is this pair:

all his tender thoughts must lie in one hole

a rat carried off her love letter this evening

The tsukeku here does make sense on its own, but most of its effect depends on its maeku. For the following tsukeku, which Senryū picked among a set of ten thousand pieces for publication in 1761, the maeku is superfluous for the tsukeku:

mottomo na koto mottomo na koto
that's understandable, that's understandable

atsusō ni hotaru o tsukamu musume no ko
as if it were hot, a young girl holds a firefly

Since the attraction of maeku-zuke lay in the original ingredients of renga, wit and humor, the subject matter tended to be "human affairs"—after all, it's difficult to be witty or funny about a landscape or weather—and some acute observations were made in senryū:

kane miseru kyaku ni morōta tameshi nashi
I've never gotten anything from a customer who shows off his
  money

~

kakoware ni jigoku wa nai to jitsu o ii
to his mistress the monk tells the truth, that there's no hell

In the original the "monk" is implied; hell, of course, is for the monk who is violating the celibacy rule by keeping a mistress.

~

yukimi to wa amari rikō na sata de nashi
snow-viewing isn't too clever a suggestion

Snow-viewing may be as poetic as flower-viewing, but, darling, why go out in this cold weather?

~

ara setai nani o yatte mo ureshigari
newlyweds are happy with whatever you give them

~

Yoshinā no hikui wa sukoshi dekikakari
"Stop that," so low, something's cooking between them

~

ryōrinin kyaku ni naru hi wa kuchi ga sugi
the day he's a customer a cook gets too critical

~

hito ni mono tada yaru ni sae jōzu heta
just giving things away, some do it well, some don't

Scholarship on Bashō's poetry and the addition of a new genre were two beneficial results of the popularity of haikai after Bashō; but the popularity may also have contributed to the enduring sense of familiarity with the 5-7-5–syllable pattern.

To backtrack somewhat, there was another spin-off from haikai no renga: haibun, prose written in a haikai spirit. Bashō was the first to set it aside as a distinct genre. A haibun may consist of a few sentences; or it may be as long as Bashō's travel diary *Oku no Hosomichi*. It often incorporates hokku. Asō Isoji, a modern scholar, has identified the following "attitudes" as characteristic of typical haibun: (1) an attempt to see "humor" in natural phenomena and human affairs because, as a Buddhist precept says, "All is void"; (2) a suave mind that sees sophisticated simplicity in things; (3) an attempt to delight serenely in "flowers, birds, the wind, and the moon"; (4) an attempt to transcend worldliness and savor an eremitic state of mind; (5) an attempt to immerse oneself in this "floating world" (*ukiyo*) and seek "elegance" (*ga*) in it; (6) an attempt to delight in eccentricity and "poetic dementia" (*fūkyō*); and (7) an attempt to see "supreme quietness" (*kanjaku*) in everything. These "attitudes" also explain much of the hokku written after Bashō.

Unfortunately, none of this made up for the debility of haikai poetry. One symptom of the malaise is an increasing practice known as *waki-okoshi,* in which a sequence was begun using a hokku of a famous poet of the past. All the renga sequences in *Asakarishū* (Hemp-Gathering Collection), for example, are waki-okoshi using Bashō's pieces. Even though the collection was intended to commemorate the hundredth anniversary of the poet's death, Bashō himself did not leave a single such sequence.

Toward the end of the nineteenth century, Masaoka Shiki (1867–1902), in discussing Bashō and his hokku, observed as follows:

"Someone said: The point truly to be savored of haikai lies in haikai no renga; hokku is only a small part of it. Therefore, any discussion of Bashō should not focus on his hokku but on his renga. Is it not said that Bashō himself did not pride himself on his hokku but on his renga?

"In reply, I said: Hokku is literature; haikai no renga is not literature; therefore, I have not discussed [the latter]. Naturally, it is not that haikai no renga does not have any literary element, but that it has at the same time other elements than literary. Accordingly, in order to discuss only its literary elements, I hold that [to look at] his hokku suffices.

"Someone said further: What are the other elements than literary?

"In reply, I said: What is held to be distinctive in haikai no renga is change. Change, in my opinion, is the element other than literary. This is because this particular change is not what changes in an order and unity that remains consistent throughout, but is a change that does not skewer together what goes ahead and what comes behind but is as abrupt as moxa treatment."

These assertions by the leader of a strong reform movement at a time when new ideas and approaches from the West were seriously confronting every traditional facet of Japanese culture, proved a near death blow to the greatly attenuated form of renga, quickly reducing output to a trickle. (Interestingly enough, because of Shiki's pejorative use, the word *tsukinami*, which at that time simply meant "monthly meeting," has come to mean "commonplace, ordinary, flat." However, he did not downgrade or notice the group-orientation of literary composition. Instead, he held countless meetings, thereby perpetuating and legitimizing the long-established tradition. Today haiku poets, like tanka poets, tend to form groups and meet regularly to write poems.)

Haikai no renga has never ceased to be composed since

Shiki's time, but attempts have been scattered. The most recent collection, called *Kasen* and published in 1981, contains three thirty-six-part sequences written in traditional style and archaic language by four prominent men of letters. Though one participant does try to introduce contemporary elements, such as Marilyn Monroe, the book is what one might expect it to be—an intellectual exercise.

An earlier publication called *Kai: Renshi,* published in 1979, is more significant. It prints linked poems in the language of today, written by members of a poetry group known as Kai (Oars). Nine of the thirteen sequences consist of thirty-six parts; the remaining four, of eighteen. The only other traditional rules followed are "disjunctive linking"—the essential rule—and incorporation of parts mentioning "flower" and "moon." In other respects the sequences are non-traditional and experimental. In the manner of most modern poetry, syllabic counts are not used. A fixed number of lines for each part, ranging from one to five, is tried in each sequence (except the first sequence where the length of each part wildly fluctuates from one to twenty-two lines). The sentiments expressed are mostly contemporary, although, in the way of renga, some allusion to classical literature is inevitable. These sequences, the first of which dates from 1972, were attempted in large part, I think, in reaction to the academic emphasis that began to be placed on renga in the 1960s. To some extent they are also attempts to see what can be done to get away from the self-absorption of the modern poet. More sequences must be written for the reader to be able to assess *Kai: Renshi* properly. But the book is surely a pioneering effort.

CHAPTER FOUR

From Hokku to Haiku

To decide when hokku, the opening part of a renga sequence, became haiku is, in a way, easy. Although the term haiku seems to date from 1663, it displaced the term hokku only when Shiki dissociated hokku from renga, dismissing the collaborative form as non-literature. The same point is made by the argument that hokku should not be thought to have become independent as long as its parent poetic form, renga, remained active—namely, until the second half of the nineteenth century.

The task of deciding the question becomes difficult when the transition is considered from the viewpoint of the evolution of the 5-7-5–syllable form. It was felt from early on that the hokku was to stand on its own; as early as 1221 it was asserted that the "hokku should make a complete statement." Reflecting that view, renga anthologies from the beginning set aside a section for hokku, and the relative importance of such sections grew. In the *Tsukubashū,* compiled in 1356, hokku took up less than six percent of the anthology; in the *Enokoshū* (Puppy's Collection), the Danrin school's 1663 anthology, the proportion was more than sixty percent; in the Bashō school's 1691 anthology *Sarumino* (Monkey's Raincoat), four hundred seventeen hokku were chosen for a selection of only four complete thirty-six-part sequences. True, nearly all of the one hundred nineteen hokku in the *Tsukubashū* were taken from those that actually opened renga sequences, but it is safe to assume that the majority of hokku in the *Enokoshū* and *Sarumino* were not. Furthermore, there are indications that Bashō often regarded the hokku as an independent poetic form. The first book he edited, *Kai Ōi* (Shell Matches, 1672), consisted of thirty pairs of matched hokku. In the already quoted portion of his letter of 1690, the phrase *haikai hokku* (in the original) evidently means "haikai no renga *and* hokku" and suggests their separation. Likewise, Morikawa Kyoriku (1656–1715) and Kawano Riyū (1662–1705) report that when someone said, "Bashō is good at *hokku;* his *haikai* is dated," Bashō responded by saying, "As for *hokku,* many among my disciples do pieces not inferior to mine. *Haikai* is where I toil [i.e., excel]." It is said that by the first decades of the eighteenth century poets had appeared who wrote hokku without any experience in renga. So, hokku began to be written more or less like haiku long before Shiki, but just when that happened is hard to pinpoint.

Is it possible to see any difference between hokku written for opening renga sequences and hokku written independently? Not, at least, in Bashō's case. The hokku that begins a renga has three requirements: it must be a complete statement; it must incorporate a word indicating the season of the time of writing; and it must be salutatory. Of these, the salutatory element may be regarded as the only candidate for deletion in a hokku not intended for a renga sequence. But its presence or absence cannot easily be made the basis for distinguishing the two kinds of hokku, because at that stage little effort was made to make the distinction and because much of salutatory rhetoric is highly refracted. Consider the following two groups of hokku by Bashō:

I

Taka hitotsu mitsukete ureshi Irago Saki
Finding a hawk, I'm delighted at Irago Point

~

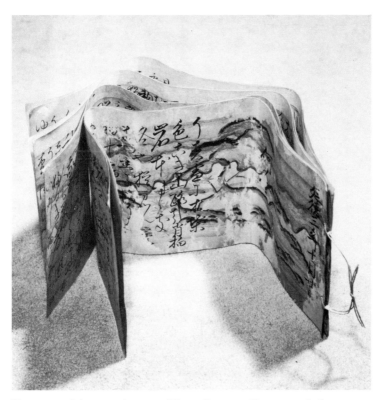

Transcript of the renga known as Three Poets at Yuyama, *which was composed on the twentieth day of the tenth month, 1491, by Shōhaku, Sochō, and Sōgi. This is believed to be one of the earliest copies showing the sequence in its original format. Collection of Kazehaya Kiuemon, Kobe. (See page 26.)*

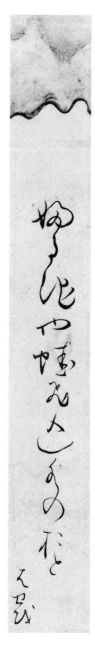

Bashō's hokku Furuike ya kawazu tobikomu mizu no oto *written in the poet's own hand and signed.* Kakie Library, Itami.

Kutabirete yado karu koro ya fuji no hana
About the time I was tired out and reached an inn—wisteria in bloom

~

Shihō yori hana fukiirete Nio no Umi
From the four directions blossoms blow into the Lake of Grebes

~

Yuku haru o Ōmi no hito to oshimikeru
Departing spring—I mourn it along with people of Ōmi

~

Meigetsu ya mon ni sashikuru shio-gashira
Bright moon: up to my gate laps the tip of the tides

II

Hana ni asobu abu na kurai so tomo suzume
Don't eat the gadfly playing in the flowers, sparrow, my friend

~

Uguisu ya mochi ni fun suru en no saki
A warbler shits on the rice cake at the end of the porch

~

Kangiku ya konuka no kakaru usu no hata
A winter chrysanthemum near a mortar's flour-sprinkled rim

~

Natsu no yo ya kuzurete akeshi hiyashi mono
The summer night has collapsed into daybreak and cold food

~

Aki mo haya baratsuku ame ni tsuki no nari
Autumn already—pattering rain and the shapes of the moon

Which group of hokku opened renga sequences? The answer is the second group, even though each hokku in the first group has a readily recognizable salutatory element, while apparently no hokku in the second does. The second piece in the second group provides a good case for understanding the refractive nature of salutation in hokku. The effect of this hokku largely draws on a haikai twist. Since the preface to the *Kokinshū* listed the "warbler singing in the flowers" as something that stirs poetic thoughts, only the vocal aspect of this songbird had been admitted in court poetry; the mention of its bowel movement, therefore, was haikai. That is to say, the description is not at all meant to express disgust. What in it is salutatory? The warbler, a kigo, is the harbinger of spring, and like the rice cake made to celebrate the coming of the new year (which by the lunar calendar began in that season), was felicitous. The idea expressed in the hokku, then, is that the spring weather is so balmy even a warbler has flown out of his bush and dropped a compliment on a rice cake put out on the porch to sun. Bashō used this hokku to begin a kasen with Kagami Shikō (1665–1731), and Shikō's waki was:

> *hi mo massugu ni hiru no atataka*
> with sunlight straight, the day is warm

Still, as long as one keeps in mind that Tohō listed this warbler hokku, along with the one on a pond and a frog, as manifesting the true spirit of haikai, a salutatory element can serve as a yardstick in differentiating the two kinds of hokku. In his treatise on haikai, Kyorai quotes the following hokku by Sakagami Kōshun (1649–1707):

> *Tsukidasu ya toi no tsumari no hikigaeru*
> Thrust out: what clogged the gutter was a toad

Kyorai then says, "I hear that [Kōshun] regards this as comparable to our dead teacher's old-pond-frog. [Kōshun's] subject is fresh, and no other piece deals with a similar idea. It must have impressed him, struck him as amusing. Nevertheless, this can hardly be made a hokku." The crucial last statement is cryptic, but Kyorai probably meant the piece lacked a salutatory element and could not be used to open a renga sequence. (In contrast, Bashō's hokku could easily be a compliment to a hermit.)

A few generations after Bashō, the hokku of a renga began to be called a *tateku*, "raising part," and an independent one, *ji-hokku*. (*Ji* here means "ground, solid," as when opposed to *mon*, "design.") Through this interval and thereafter, salutation was neglected in independent hokku (expect those written for celebratory purposes) in favor of other effects. Yosa Buson, for example, was fond of creating novelistic atmospheres:

Koi-wataru Kamakura bushi no ōgi kana
In prolonged love, that Kamakura warrior with his fan

~

Toba-dono e gorokki isogu nowaki kana
Toward the Toba Palace several horsemen rush through the
field-cleaver

In the first piece, a Kamakura warrior (long a thing of the past) is described as going about with effeminate accounterments like a fan, in a vain attempt to look nice, now that he is hopelessly in love. This is funny because Kamakura warriors were reputed to be rough, tough, and rustic. In the second, the Toba Palace is a large palace complex built by the emperors Shirakawa (1053–1129) and Toba (1103–58) during a period that experienced many military disturbances. So, horsemen hurrying toward the palace in a stormy gust ("field-cleaver") suggest another upheaval. Both hokku, of course, give imagined pictures, rather than actually observed scenes.

Kobayashi Issa (1763–1827) was, among other things, fascinated by lively movements and tried to reproduce them:

Ta ni hata ni tenten mai no kochō kana
Over paddies and fields flurrying dots of butterflies

~

Doka-doka to hana no ue naru bafun kana
Thud-thud upon the flowers drops the horse turd

~

Shiratsuyu ni zabu to fumikomu karasu kana
Splashing the white dew, a crow steps in

Issa's concern with descriptive accuracy brings us back to Shiki, who, impressed by Western drawing techniques, proposed to "sketch" natural phenomena objectively. By then haikai had degraded into *fūryū inji,* which may be translated "petty transcendentalism and worthless poetizing." Coming along with his assertion that the hokku had to be separated from renga, Shiki's proposal sounded a fresh note and became the credo of his school. After his death, his school split into two factions, and each of the two in time fragmented further. As I will describe in more detail in chapter 6, some poets began writing pieces disregarding syllabic patterns and counts, and others began breaking up the form that was traditionally printed in one line into several lines. But the predominant concern of the haiku poet since Shiki—and to some extent since Bashō—has remained more or less the same: to be faithful to one's perception.

What follows is a chronological selection of hokku and haiku, mainly on the frog, from the time of Bashō to the present. (The number of syllables is given at right when the piece is hypermetric or hypometric.)

Matsuo Bashō (1644–94)

Furuike ya kawazu tobikomu mizu no oto
An old pond: a frog jumps in—the sound of water

Takarai Kikaku (1661–1707)

Amagaeru bashō ni norite soyogi keri
A tree frog rides a plantain leaf, wavering

Mukai Kyorai (1651–1704)

Ta no aze ya niji o seoite naku kawazu
On the paddy-divider, a rainbow on his back, a frog croaks

Naitō Jōsō (1662–1704)

Toritsukanu chikara de ukamu kawazu kana
With the strength that does not cling, a frog floats

Sugiyama Sampū (1647–1732)

Samidare ni kawazu no oyogu toguchi kana
In these May rains frogs swim near my door

Ochi Etsujin (1656–1739)

Akatsuki o mutsukashi sō ni naku kawazu
At daybreak, as if with difficulty, frogs croak

Hattori Tohō (1657–1730)

Mizukusa no kawazu karabiru hideri kana
On the waterweeds frogs lie parched in this drought

Chiyojo (1703–75)

Amagumo ni hara no fukururu kawazu kana
At the rainclouds the frog's belly becomes full

Tan Taigi (1709–71)

Kawazu ite naku ya ukimo no ue to shita
Frogs must be there croaking, above and below the floating
weeds

Yosa Buson (1716–83)

Kaku ni zashite tōku kawazu o kiku yo kana   [18]
Seated in his pavilion he listens to distant frogs during the night

Miyake Shōzan (1718–1801)

Majimaji to shite wa kawazu no arukikeri
Every now and then the frog stares and then walks

Takakuwa Rankō (1726–98)

Kawazu naku ta no mizu ugoku tsukiyo kana
Frogs croak, the paddy water moves, this moonlit night

Katō Kyōtai (1732–92)

Mizuumi no mizu naki kobosu kawazu kana
From the water of the lake the croaks spill of those frogs

Kaya Shirao (1738?–91)

Okifushi ni toko no hiki ou yamome kana
Getting up, a widow shoos away a toad from her bed

Natsume Seibi (1749–1816)

Kawazu naku soba made asaru suzume kana
Right up to the croaking frogs sparrows forage

Iida Atsuoi (died 1826)

Mioboe no kawazu tobu nari niwa no ame
A frog I remember seeing leaps in the garden's rain

Tagawa Hōrō (1726–1845)

Nakanu ma mo nodo no tada inu kawazu kana
Even while not croaking the frog's throat doesn't stay idle

Kobayashi Issa (1763–1827)

Mukimuki ni kawazu no itoko hatoko kana
Every way he turns the frog has cousins, second cousins

Sakurai Baishitsu (1769–1852)

Ko o motte shizuka na mono wa kawazu kana
Have a child, and what's so quiet are those frogs

Masaoka Shiki (1867–1902)

Mon shimeni dete kiite oru kawazu kana
Coming out to close the gate I end up listening to frogs

Takahama Kyoshi (1874–1959)

Kogi idete kawazu kikoezu narinikeri
Having rowed out I have ceased to hear the frogs

Kawahigashi Hekigodō (1873–1937)

Yadokari umi ni tsubushite modorikeri   [16]
Hermit crab; I crushed it in the sea and came away

Nakatsukasa Ippekirō (1887–1946)

Naru gotoku kawazu naku yo no suguki michi
As if roaring, frogs croak along night's straight road

Ogiwara Seisensui (1884–1976)

mushi naku naka ni mushi naku   [11]
amid insects chirping insects chirp

Ozaki Hōsai (1885–1926)

suzume no atatakasa nigiri hanashite yaru   [18]
I grip the sparrow's warmth let it go

Murakami Kijō (1865–1938)

Fuyu-bachi no shini dokoro naku arukikeri
A winter wasp, without a place to die, walks

Iida Dakotsu (1885–1962)

Fuyu no hiki kawa ni hanateba oyogikeri
A winter toad, as I release it in the river, swims

Hara Sekitei (1886–1951)

Kaeru no ko hitotsu koku dete asobikeri
One tadpole detaches itself, dark, and is playing

Sugita Hisajo (1890–1946)

Kami no ka no ikiruru yo kana naku kawazu
Hair's fragrance stifling tonight, frogs croak

Mizuhara Shūōshi (born 1892)

Kawazu ta no kururu ososa yo ame no ato
How slowly the frog paddies darken after the rain

Yamaguchi Seishi (born 1901)

Kage o dete hikari ni utaru agehachō
Out of the shadow, struck by the light, a swallowtail

Yamaguchi Seison (born 1892)

Hito o shinji kawazu no uta o kiki itari   [18]
Trusting in people I am listening to the songs of frogs

Nakamura Kusatao (born 1901)

Aki no hae hitotsu mamizu no ue ni shisu
An autumn fly, just one, dies on the pure water

Katō Shūson (born 1905)

Hiki aruku kuso ryō yo ni mo takumashiku
A toad walks its shit volume out of this world powerful

Ishida Hakyō (born 1912)

Ruirui to hiki tsurumi shujutsu nobite ori   [18]
One upon the other toads mate, my operation's dragging on

Saitō Sanki (1900–1962)

Yawarakaki semi umarekite iwa tsukamu [18]
A soft cicada, born and out, clutches the rock

Taneda Santōka (1882–1940)

mizu no umasa o kaeru naku [12]
water's sweet the frogs croak

Mitsuhashi Takajo (1899–1972)

Enten ni kanashimi aeri tsuru to hito
Under burning heaven, pitying each other, crane and woman

Tomizawa Kakio (1902–62)

Hebi yogiru ikusa ni areshi waga manako
A snake crosses my battle-ravaged eyes

Nomiyama Asuka (1917–70)

Futo ware no shigai ni uji no takaru miyu
Suddenly I see my corpse infested with maggots

Hashimoto Takako (1899–1963)

Tōchō mo kioku no chō mo hane o kaki
Both frozen butterfly and butterfly in my memory lack their
wings

Shinohara Bon (born 1910)

Ame mae no kuraki ni hikari kaeru iru
Gleaming in the dark before rain a frog sits

Akao Tōshi (born 1925)

kaeru sakare penki ya no mado no kuragari [18]
frog torn the painter's shop window's darkness

Iida Ryūta (born 1920)

Ō-goi no kabane mi ni yuku ite no naka
I go to see the cadaver of a large carp in the freeze

Ishihara Yatsuka (born 1919)

Yami nareba hitori waraeri hiki ga naki
Because of the darkness alone I laugh, a toad croaks

Kadokawa Gen'yoshi (1917–75)

Tennō no hi kaeru chiisaki koe tatsuru   [18]
On Emperor's Day frogs raise tiny voices

Katsura Nobuko (born 1914)

Hikigaeru yami no tsuzuki no yama ōte
A toad carrying a mountain contiguous to the dark

Kaneko Tōta (born 1919)

gyorai no marudō tokage hai mawarite sarinu   [20]
torpedo's round belly a lizard crawled on it and left

Kishida Chigyo (born 1918)

Kirigirisu yokujō shi mizu nomi ni yuku
Katydid: lusting I go to drink water

Kusama Tokihiko (born 1920)

Kuchi no naka yogore kittari iwashi kū
The inside of my mouth utterly foul, I eat sardines

Satō Onifusa (born 1919)

Chimamire no higashi e yuruku kan'a tobu
Toward the bloody east slackly a cold crow flies

Sawaki Kin'ichi (born 1919)

Te no hira no ayu o jotai no gotoku miru
I look at the sweetfish on my palm as at a female body

Suzuki Murio (born 1919)

Kūshū no chikazuku tsukiyo no tori o saku   [18]
An air raid coming close this moonlit night I split a chicken

Tagawa Hiryoshi (born 1914)

chō wa hishō no genkei to shite mirai made   [19]
butterfly, as the prototype of flight, into the future

Nozawa Setsuko (born 1920)

Hebi o mite hikarishi manako mochi aruku
I carry about eyes that glisten, having seen a snake

Fujita Shōshi (born 1926)

Kurage yori nishi e ikamu to omoishi nomi   [18]
Merely thought of going farther west than jellyfish do

Ameyama Minoru (born 1926)

Kotori shini kareno yoku suku kago nokoru
Bird dead, withered field transparent, cage remains

CHAPTER FIVE

Some Aspects of the Question, What Is a Haiku?

What is a haiku? This question is asked more frequently, I feel, than a similar question on, say, the sonnet or limerick. To limit the scope of our discussion to North America, a special committee of the Haiku Society of America came up with definitions of haiku in the early 1970s and they were submitted to publishers of English dictionaries. Nevertheless, only several years afterward the editor of the society's magazine felt compelled to ask a group of people to respond to the same question. More recently, the Haiku Society of Canada reviewed some observations on haiku in "A Definition of the Modern English Haiku." Meanwhile, the Western World Haiku Society, of Portland, Oregon, appears to be perpetually asking and answering the question. Why this persistent inquiry? I think there are three reasons.

For one thing, haiku is a relatively new poetic form in North America. Commodore Perry of the United States Navy went to Japan in 1853 and helped open the country to world commerce, but the first scholarly treatment in English of haiku did not appear until half a century later, in 1902, when Basil Hall Chamberlain published a monograph entitled "The Japanese Poetical Epigram." (He explained the term "epigram" as "denoting any little piece of verse that expresses a delicate or ingenious thought.") Chamberlain regarded the Japanese language as "incomparably inferior" to English and Japanese prosody as "puerile," so one wonders how imagism, with haiku as a major influence, could have begun as it did less than a decade later. There were spurts of interest in haiku after imagism, until World War II. But I think Cor van den Heuvel is right in saying in his *Haiku Anthology* that "haiku in English got its real start in the [nineteen-] fifties," when for a combination of reasons interest in Japan became less exotic and serious. The history of haiku in North America, then, is only about three decades long. It is natural that this alien poetic form, with familiarity with it so short, should continue to invite debate on its tenets.

For another, haiku as literary genre has a sharply delineated territory in Japan, where it originated. There, those who write haiku are called *haijin,* those who write 5-7-5-7-7–syllable tanka *kajin,* and those who write other forms of poetry *shijin.* And although there are some notable exceptions, each group does not usually invade another's territory. Japanese as a whole are true believers in the adage "Jack of all trades, master of none," and the three groupings reflect the Japanese poet's strong tendency to stick to the form in which he starts writing. (One English word that comes to mind in this connection is "sonneteer," but no one expects a sonneteer to write sonnets exclusively.) Probably because of these distinctions, there is an amorphous sentiment among some Japanese that "a haiku is not a poem," and they, given the chance, say so. (It is well to remember that Bashō, a typical Japanese in that he wrote almost exclusively in one form, did not regard his medium, renga, as non-poetry.)

Finally, there is the brevity of the haiku form, as well as the fact that the form comes from Japan, an Oriental country. The two go together. Haiku is short; if translated straightforwardly, the seventeen syllables should on the average come to the length of an Alexandrine. But had it originated in, say, Ireland, would the implication survive that haiku has something more than meets the eye? I doubt it.

Let us consider the second and third points further. First, the matter of territory. That those Japanese who write haiku tend to write no other forms of poetry derives, as has been noted, from the national character, but there is the concomitant matter of terminology. The word *shi,* which directly comes from the Chinese word *shih,* denotes, in classical Japanese literature, poetry written in Chinese and, in modern literature, poetry that is neither haiku nor tanka. It is this word that is usually translated "poem" or "poetry." Accordingly, when a Japanese says, "A haiku is not a poem," he is in most cases being self-evident or misleading.

This said, I must stress that efforts to identify the attributes of haiku are made in Japan. Here, the predominant voice for the last few decades has been Yamamoto Kenkichi (born 1907), who professes to write no haiku himself. His critical stand can be termed orthodox; he asserts that "haiku has not once attained to the height that it reached as the hokku of haikai no renga during Bashō's age." As might be expected, his various theories are based mostly on Bashō's writings and words ascribed to him in general and, in particular, the following passage in Tohō's *Sanzōshi* (Three Booklets):

"As for hokku, it is, philosophically, the mind that goes off and returns. For example, it is like:

Yamazato wa manzai ososhi ume no hana
In this mountain village the comedians are late: plum blossoms

"Like the state of mind that simply says, 'In this mountain village the comedians are late,' and then says, 'The plums are in bloom,' the mind that goes off and returns is what makes a hokku."

The quoted hokku is Bashō's, and the observation is believed to be his, too. From this cryptic passage, Yamamoto has constructed a theory that a haiku is an antinomical poem. From it, too, he has argued that the two essences of a haiku are *kokkei,* humor or comicality, and *aisatsu,* salutatoriness. In his analysis neither word is used in its traditional sense; *kokkei,* in his view, is generated when a reader reads a haiku, goes back to its beginning, and then—only then—understanding what the piece is all about, smiles; and *aisatsu* occurs when that smile does, for such a smile is intended as salutatory for the person who composed the haiku. Yamamoto's ideas are also based on the socio-anthropological view that Bashō's poetry was possible only in the communal setting where it came into being. Not surprisingly for such a conservative scholar, Yamamoto takes an extremely dim view of haiku that deviate from the 5-7-5–syllable pattern. What is surprising is the absence of theoretical arguments that counter Yamamoto's. But this is partly made up for by haiku that negate his propositions.

How do the brevity of the haiku and its origin in Japan affect the attempt to define haiku? The question mainly concerns those outside Japan, and when only discussions written in English are considered, the principal response to it is found in the Zen interpretation of haiku. Chamberlain, who called the seventeen-syllable form an "epigram," said that to understand the "moral signification attributed to many of Bashō's epigrams . . . a thorough study of the influence of the mysticism of the Zen sect in Japan" would be indispensable. With this, Chamberlain set the trend; most of the notable books dealing with haiku since then have stressed Zen, with Harold G. Henderson's *Introduction to Haiku*, published in 1958, as probably the major exception. The largest splash was made by R. H. Blyth with his several volumes on haiku, which have the consistent theme that "haiku is Zen." Those who followed him largely echoed him. And so, Kenneth Yasuda, in his 1957 book *The Japanese Haiku*, says, "Bashō did not consider the haiku form too 'small' to express his realizations of not-so-simple an attitude as that of Zen." In *The Wordless Poem: A Study of Zen in Haiku*, published in 1969, Eric Amann says that a "haiku is . . . a manifestation of Zen." Joan Giroux, in her 1974 book *The Haiku Form*, says, "No complete discussion of haiku is possible without mentioning Zen." In *The Haiku Anthology*, published in the same year, its editor, Cor van den Heuvel, says that a haiku "is *now* in one of those timeless moments when it flashes forth an unspoken message of the oneness of existence." In 1978 the Zen master Robert Aitken published a book called *A Zen Wave,* in which he sets forth Zen interpretations of Bashō's hokku. Interestingly enough, the definition of a haiku-like image that Ezra Pound offered in the 1920s to explain imagism strikes a startlingly similar note: "an intellectual and emotional complex in an instant of time."

To no small extent Japanese have contributed to this perception. In the middle of the nineteenth century, when they ended their self-imposed isolation that lasted two hundred and fifty years, they found themselves behind Western civilizations in various human endeavors. Their situation was rather like that of the proverbial frog in a well suddenly made aware of the vast ocean. But as the initial shock was overcome, they began upholding indigenous manifestations, and as Chamberlain noted with mild contempt and amused disbelief, they "set themselves to discover Japanese Shakespeares, Japanese Scotts, Japanese Victor Hugos, etc., etc., etc. . . . [Using imported Western terminologies, they] discover a criticism of life—the whole Zen philosophy in fact—in that single stanza of [Bashō's] on the old pond and the frog jumping into the water." Zen came in handy, because its secrets in principle remain unsaid and unwritten, thereby giving it any degree of profundity needed by its user. Japanese succeeded so well in selling Zen that by the 1920s Westerners' Zennish interpretation of haiku and other Japanese cultural phenomena reached a point where a Japanese poet, Takamura Kōtarō (1883–1956), was irritated enough to write a satirical poem intended for "European poets who amuse themselves with the Orient." It has the following lines: "With your wooly hands / you may tug at me / and try to seat me on the Great Road to cheap instant Enlightenment, / but I'll have to excuse myself." Still, the effort continued, as witness Daisetz Suzuki's treatise in the 1950s, "Zen and Haiku," with this typical observation: "a *haiku* does not express ideas but . . . puts forward images reflecting intuitions.

These images are not figurative representations made use of by the poetic mind, but . . . intuitions themselves."

In the face of such ardent desires to see Zen in haiku, any attempt to dissociate the two may be futile. But as I hope I have shown in the preceding chapters, actual hokku and haiku have little to do with Zen. Hokku and haiku have been written to congratulate, to praise, to describe, to express gratitude, wit, cleverness, disappointment, resentment, or what have you, but rarely to convey enlightenment. Indeed, any piece intended for this last purpose would be a contradiction in terms; as Satō Madoka (born 1909) says in his book on Bashō's relation to Zen, Zen exists in its rejection of verbal media, whereas literature, including poetry, cannot exist without them. Satō does say that Bashō's hokku on the old pond and a frog is "Zenlike" but strongly doubts that the poet was enlightened. Bashō himself, in his only hokku that directly bears on the subject of Zen, seems to express great wariness of enlightenment:

A certain wise man said to me, "Undigested Zen and undigested Buddhism—they are hell":

Inazuma ni satoranu hito no tōtosa yo
Someone not enlightened by lightning—how venerable!

PART TWO

TRANSLATING INTO ENGLISH

CHAPTER SIX

Translating Hokku, Haiku, and Renga

In translating hokku, haiku, and renga I try, as with literature in any form, to remain as faithful to the original as I can. In content, this means I try not to add or change words. The temptation to add words is considerable. The nature and the brevity of these forms—a renga is basically a series of short poems—make many pieces allusive, cryptographic, and elliptic. The extent of the difficulty may be guessed from the fact that Buson already found "incomprehensible" most hokku by Kikaku, who was active only seventy years or so earlier. Also, much of the subject matter of this genre seems culturally too limited to be transferred to another language without explication, although, here, the problem may be less cross-cultural than literary: many seasonal and other references in classical hokku are lost to the modern Japanese reader. I think both the intrinsic and cultural difficulties are more imagined than real. When they exist, however, they should be explained in a note, not in the translation. Adding explanatory words in translation strikes me as a fallacy, even where the poet's own explanation might seem to make it justifiable.

The temptation to change words is no less great. Even though haikai no renga revolutionized poetic diction, much of haikai diction was standardized, as is typically shown by kigo. Standardized diction is also common, if to a lesser degree, in modern haiku, especially those that follow orthodox approaches. Accordingly, someone who decides to work on a substantial number of hokku or haiku, rather than a randomly picked few or a whole renga sequence, must also decide whether or not to translate the same word or phrase in the same way all the time. Bashō, for example, wrote at least ten hokku incorporating the word *meigetsu,* the moon that appears on the fifteenth of the eighth month and a popular kigo for autumn. To give another example, Bashō used the more or less abstract word *koe,* "voice," to describe the quacking of ducks (*Umi kurete kamo no koe honokani shiroshi*), the chirping of cicadas (*Shizukasa ya iwa ni shimiiru semi no* koe), and the guokking of a night heron (*Inazuma ya yami no kata yuku goi no* koe), among others. Should one stick to the English word one has chosen for the same word or phrase? I think I should, although I often fail to.

In form, faithfulness to the original means two things to me. First, on the average my translations must come to about seventy percent of the original poems in syllabic count, which is twelve syllables in the case of those written in the orthodox 5-7-5–syllable form. Second, I translate hokku and haiku into one line, except where lineation is specified by the poet. The former, the quantitative point, is something I found while translating for money and have since loosely used as a yardstick. My yardstick is indirectly supported by an observation made by the Haiku Society of America committee to define haiku terminology: that by 1970 more writers of English-language haiku were composing haiku of fewer than seventeen syllables. The observation suggests that writers of haiku in English came to feel what is perceived to be haiku-esque should be expressed in less than seventeen syllables in English. To put it differently, to impose in translation a 5-7-5–syllable pattern or a form that approximates it may dilute and render ineffectual what is haiku-esque.

The latter point, lineation, requires some historical explanation. Before the middle of the nineteenth century, when modern printing techniques began to be used in Japan, hokku and senryū, despite their syllabic patterns of 5-7-5, were printed in one line, although they were broken up in various lines when they were written on fans, *tanzaku* (oblong poem cards), *shiki-shi* (more or less square poem cards), as part of a *haiga* (haikai painting), or for other aesthetic presentations. The practice of printing seventeen-syllable pieces in one line was continued when they began to be typeset. If that were still the sole practice, translating hokku, senryū, and haiku in three lines might be justified as a means of emphasizing their distinct syllabic patterns. But a few things have happened since the days of Shiki. They are the development of *jiyū-ritsu* or "free rhythm" haiku that ignore syllable counts; the related development of *tanshi*, short poems, and *tanshō*, short pieces, both of which may best be described as one-line poems; and the appearance of haiku poets who use punctuation, space, and lineation.

One way of understanding these phenomena is to describe the history of modern haiku in conventional fashion. Shiki, who gave currency to the term "haiku," is considered the first modern haiku poet because of his advocacy of faithfulness to what is observed, though he stuck to the 5-7-5–syllable form. Here are some of his haiku:

Nanohana ya patto akaruki machi hazure
Rape flowers flash to brightness the edge of the town

~

Waka-ayu no futate ni narite agarikeri
Young sweetfish turn into two groups and go upstream

~

Kaki kueba kane ga narunari Hōryū-ji
I eat a persimmon and the bell rings at the Hōryū-ji

~

Yūkaze ya shiro bara no hana mina ugoku
In the evening wind blooming white roses all stir

~

Keitō no jūshigo hon mo arinu beshi
Cockscombs—there's got to be fourteen or fifteen of them

Shiki regarded as outstanding two men among those who studied with him: Kawahigashi Hekigodō (1873–1937), who was, he said, "cool as water," and Takahama Kyoshi (1874–1959), who was "as hot as fire." Shiki was uncannily right in his estimates; the two men later became the heads of two opposing branches of haiku philosophy.

Hekigodō inherited from Shiki the editorship of the haiku column of the newspaper *Nippon* (Japan) and while vigorously stressing Shiki's ideal of faithfulness to what is observed, restlessly pursued newness. He welcomed experiment, abandoned syllabic counts, began to call his pieces "poems," and in the end "retired" from the haiku world. Here are some of his pieces written after he dropped the 5-7-5–syllable form (syllable counts follow in brackets):

kumo no mine inaho no hashiri   [12]
peaks of clouds the ears of rice stalks run

~

Enoshima modori ga fukimakuru samusa ni natte shimaeri   [24]
the returner from Enoshima has ended up becoming the swirling
   cold

~

sutōbu ni yori mono iwane domo ware wa oya nari   [21]
leaning to a stove and saying nothing but I am your parent

~

   Paris
metoro ni agatta yoru no kaze no ha no oto ni naruru   [22]
coming up the Metro the night wind the sound of leaves I've
   become used to

Among those who were sympathetic to Hekigodō's causes, Ogiwara Seisensui (1884–1976) was a few years ahead of him in writing haiku that are not based on seventeen syllables and went a step further by discarding kigo. For the rest of his long life Seisensui did not swerve from these principles. It was through his efforts and the magazine he began in 1911, *Sōun* (Strati), that two names came to be known: Ozaki Hōsai

(1885–1926), in my opinion the best modern haiku poet, and Taneda Santōka (1882–1940), who has become immensely popular in Japan during the past decade. Seisensui was also the first to attempt lineation in print. In 1914 he included the following two-line haiku in the first selection from *Sōun*:

chikara ippai ni naku ko to
naku tori to no asa   [20]

with all their might a child cries
and a rooster cries this morning

~

wazuka no hana ga chirikereba
ume wa sōmi ni meguminu   [23]

the few blossoms having scattered
the plum has budded all over its body

~

aozora ni tobitaki fūsen o
shika to motsu sena no ko yo   [24]

into the blue sky the balloon wants to fly up,
you hold it tight on my back, child

It is said that Seisensui began writing haiku in two lines under the influence of the couplets of Goethe and Schiller and in the belief that a haiku consists of two parts with a pause between them. But he did not lineate many haiku, or for long, and when he included the two-line haiku in his first collection in 1920, he put them into one line.

True haiku lineators, ironically, came out of the formalist wing of Shiki's tradition, led by his other protégé, Kyoshi. When Shiki died and Hekigodō became the haiku editor of *Nippon*, Kyoshi became the de facto proprietor of *Hototogisu* (Cuckoo), a haiku magazine begun in 1897. But for the next ten years he concentrated on prose, causing an alarming drop in the number of subscribers to the magazine and in its influence. In the 1910s he decided to go back to haiku. A remark he made in 1912 has become famous: "What I understand as haiku is a kind of classical literature. . . . Classical literature means a special literature that has been under certain restrictions from the days of old. . . . What are the restrictions of haiku? To mention a couple of major ones, they are preference for kigo, the limit on the syllabic number to seventeen, and poetic tone."

Kyoshi's remark was intended to counter the influence of Hekigodō and his sympathizers, but its timing coincided with the period when the latter group began to fragment. Kyoshi's grip on the haiku world thereafter is usually described as "dictatorial." Nevertheless, there were inevitable "actions and reactions" among his ranks. One important reaction occurred in 1931 when Mizuhara Shūōshi (born 1892), a prominent contributor to *Hototogisu,* broke away and began his own magazine. Shūōshi's move was in protest to Kyoshi's growing stress on objective faithfulness to nature, and it touched off a movement soon to be known as *shinkō haiku,* which may be freely translated "new-wave haiku." It was in that movement, eventually, that Tomizawa Kakio (1902–62) came to write haiku using space or a dash to indicate a pause in a line, such as:

enrai ya   yugami ni utsuru uo no kao   [17]
far-off rumble   mirrored in a distortion a fish's face

~

ama no kawa   futo   kyōon   no tsumazukinu   [17]
River of Heaven   abruptly   a footfall   stumbles

~

ryūboku—keijijōteki na—kuroi kyori   [17]
driftwood—metaphysical—black distance

And a man fascinated by Kakio, Takayanagi Shigenobu (born 1923), became the first important haiku lineator. The number of lines he uses ranges from one to fifteen, the number of syllables often exceeding seventeen. As might be expected of a poet with such an approach, Shigenobu also uses an array of typographical devices: variegated indentation; alignment at the bottom, which is comparable to alignment at right in English; space between lines, which appears to be a stanzaic break at times; parentheses; dots. (Typeface variations may be the only device he has not used.) Here are some of his haiku:

mi o sorasu niji no
zetten
      shokeidai   [17]

body arched rainbow's
pinnacle
      the gallows

~

fune yakisuteshi
senchō wa

oyogu kana   [17]

having burned his ship
the captain

is swimming

~

tsui ni
      tanima ni
miidasaretaru
momoiro hanabi   [21]

finally
      in the valley
it has been found
pink firework

~

sanmyaku no
     hida ni
          ki
          ki
          su
          mi
     umo
      re
      ru
    mimi
     ra   [19]

to the mountain range's
              folds
          listen-
              ing
            lim-
           pidly

          those
           bur-
            ied
           ear
             s

   More recently Morimoto Norio (born 1917), another poet
from the formalist wing of Shiki's tradition, has published a
collection of what he chooses to call *saitanshi,* shortest poems.
Though he says his "saitanshi are no longer haiku," they are,
nevertheless, based on his belief that the haiku is "the shortest
poem in the world."

kami wa
umi no
nioi   [9]

your hair
smells of
the sea

~

tabetsukusarenai
seiyoku   [12]

I can't eat all this
lust

~

shiro wa
yami no ue   [8]

the castle
is above the darkness

~

noboritsumete
tentōmushi wa
mata
hikikaesu   [20]

climbing to the top
the ladybug
again
turns back

As Shigenobu has pointed out, haiku lineators are a minority;
there is a strong pull to one-line form. (The same is true of
5-7-5-7-7–syllable tanka. I have discussed tanka lineation in
"Translating Tanka in One-Line Form," *Montemora,* no. 4,
1978, pp. 178–80.) Still, the existence of lineated pieces and
the belief shared by the majority that one line is the standard
seem to justify following the lineation of the original in print.

If the reasoning so far has some validity, lineation in renga translation does not require an extensive comment. When classical renga sequences were printed each of the 5-7-5– and 7-7–syllable parts was apparently given as one line, and modern texts follow this practice. I translate 5-7-5–syllable hokku into one line, and so render 7-7–syllable parts into another line. Ideally I should be able to alternate long and short lines, although my emphasis on the literal sense of the original sometimes prevents me from achieving this pattern.

The problem renga poses for a translator is highly technical, and it directly arises from the form's basic structure. As we have seen, any set of three consecutive parts, A, B, and C, in a renga sequence requires the relation of part C to part B to differ radically from that of part B to part A. In other words, a renga is a sequence in which the narrative thread must be broken at every other turn. This requirement was no doubt fostered by a language with which one can make a seemingly conclusive statement that leaves unspecified the number, gender, sentence subject, and other particulars of its components. Consideration of this has persuaded some translators to give two different versions of each part in rendering a renga into English. But here again, I think the difficulty is more imagined than real.

Let us look at an example from *Tobi no Ha mo* (A Kite's Feathers, Too), a kasen that Bashō composed in 1690 with Kyorai, Nozawa Bonchō (died 1714), and Nakamura Fumikuni (dates uncertain):

25 *uki hito o kikoku-gaki yori kugurasen*   Bashō

26 *ima ya wakare no katana sashidasu*   Kyorai

27 *sewashige ni kushi de kashira o kakichirashi*   Bonchō

28 *omoikittaru shinigurui miyo*   Fumikuni

29 *seiten ni ariake-zuki no asaborake*   Kyorai

A renga annotator enjoys as much leeway as a director of a play, or greater perhaps, and this passage, like any other, is subject to divergent interpretations. It is generally agreed, however, that part 25 suggests a remark of a noblewoman thinking of letting her lover in through a hedge; that part 26 describes a mistress, possibly a courtesan, parting with her lover in the morning; that part 27 describes a harried wage earner at a brothel, or a warrior—in either case, an indoor scene; that part 28 is either a defiant statement of a warrior preparing for battle or an observation of someone looking at a warrior slaughtered in the frenzy of battle; and that part 29 describes a landscape at dawn. Taking these interpretative possibilities into account, Earl Miner, an American authority on renga, has translated this passage as follows:

25   His neglect was heartless
      but he went again to visit her
        through the mock-orange hedge
26 now is the time of lovers' parting
    and she helps him put on his sword

    At the time of lovers' parting
    she helped him put on his sword
27   left all restless
      with her comb she worried her hair
        messing its lines

    In a restless state
    with his comb he worries his hair
      messing its lines
28 summoning determination
    to hazard his life in battle

    He summoned determination
    to hazard his life in battle
29   in the chill blue sky
      the yet remaining moon dissolves
        in the light of dawn

Judging someone else's translation is difficult, especially when it involves an approach or theory, rather than a choice of words or a difference in interpretation. Still, as I said to Mr. Miner in our discussion of his book *Japanese Linked Poetry* (*Journal of the Association of Teachers of Japanese* 14, no. 2, 1979, pp. 181–93), I doubt if translating the same verse twice, the second time differently, is necessary or appropriate. Evidently Mr. Miner's translations clarify each image and the way it changes its meaning as it relates to the foregoing and following parts. However, it seems to me, the arrangement Mr. Miner has devised slows down the reading, limits the scope of interpretation, and lessens the ambiguity of the original. I would prefer translations that are less explicatory and more concise. Here is my translation of the same passage:

25 "He's the one who saddens me—I'll let him through the syringa hedge"

26   now at parting she hands him his sword

27 hair hurriedly scratched with a comb

28   "Look at this determined death struggle!"

29 daybreak moon in the blue sky, as the morning comes

Mr. Miner's translation and mine are two extremes. Fortunately, this renga, *Tobi no Ha mo,* is among the most translated. Those interested can read the versions by R. H. Blyth in volume 1 of *Haiku* (Tokyo: Hokuseido Press, 1949–52; pp. 131–34), by the Nippon Gakujutsu Shinkōkai in *Haikai and Haiku* (Tokyo: Nippon Gakujutsu Shinkōkai, 1958; pp. 95–105), by Geoffrey Bownas and Anthony Thwaite in *The Penguin Book of Japanese Verse* (Harmondsworth and Baltimore: Penguin Books, 1964; pp. 124–27), by Cana Maeda in *Monkey's Raincoat* (New York: Mushinsha/Grossman Publishers, 1973; pp. 35–43), and by Etsuko Terasaki in "Hatsushigure" (*Harvard Journal of Asiatic Studies* 36, 1976, pp.223–3 8). My translation is found in *From the Country of Eight Islands,* translated with Burton Watson (Garden City, New York: Doubleday and Company; Seattle: University of Washington Press, 1981, pp. 300–303).

~•~ CHAPTER SEVEN ~•~
One Hundred Frogs

Some time ago, while exchanging elephant and other jokes with me, Kyoko Selden sent a list of about twenty English and French translations of Bashō's hokku *Furuike ya kawazu tobikomu mizu no oto* and asked if I could identify the translators. I managed only a couple of guesses, all wrong. Then it occurred to me to see how many English translations there are of this famous set of seventeen syllables. Shiki once said, "Even among those under heaven who don't have the faintest idea what haikai is, there is no one who doesn't recite this piece on an old pond, and at the mention of 'hokku' they at once think of the old pond." As befits a literary piece so widely known, and so short, far more translations have been found than I had expected.

Word for word, *furuike* is a noun made up of the adjective *furushi* (old) and the noun *ike* (pond, pool, or mere) and means a pond that has existed for a time. About *ya,* a kireji, much has been said and written both in Japan and elsewhere. Commenting on this and two other well-known kireji, Harold J. Isaacson says in *Peonies Kana: Haiku by the Upasaka Shiki,* published in 1972, that "they have the meaning that lies in themselves as sounds, and in that way are as meaningful when set in the English translation as they are in the Japanese." But by Bashō's time eighteen kireji had been recognized, and Bashō himself simply said, "Every sound unit is a kireji."

Kawazu (frog) can be either singular or plural because, as here, the Japanese language rarely makes numeral distinctions.

Bashō's own picture illustrates the hokku with a single frog and, besides, the Zen overtones ascribed to the hokku may favor a one-frog interpretation. Also, the hokku is "matched" with one that suggests a single frog rather than many. In *Kawazu Awase* (Frog Matches), a collection of forty-one hokku judged in pairs (there was one extra one, yes) in the intercalary third month of 1686, it was paired with a hokku by Senka (seventeenth century):

Itaike ni kawazu tsukubau ukiha kana
Innocently a frog squats on a floating leaf

Then too, as seldom happens, some Japanese commentators have brought up the question of number and agreed on a single frog.

But all this does not annul the image of many frogs. The argument for more than one frog may be supported, first, by the actual existence of the pond to which Bashō may have referred. It is known that Sugiyama Sampū (1647–1732), a rich fish merchant, gave Bashō a house around which were ponds stocked with fish, and it is hard to imagine the pond Bashō may have had in mind as the exclusive residence of a hermit frog. In addition, some entries in *Kawazu Awase* are indisputably about more than one frog. For example, the hokku by Kyorai reads:

Hito-aze wa shibashi nakiyamu kawazu kana
One paddy ceases croaking for a while—the frogs

In the end, though, what makes the argument for two or more frogs possible is the ambiguity of the language.

Singular or plural, *kawazu* is the subject of the verb that follows, *tobikomu* (to jump or leap in), here, as happens in Japanese grammar, at once the conclusive and the noun-modifying form. The final five syllables, *mizu no oto* (water's sound) are not, as sometimes translated, onomatopoeic.

A version of the hokku, with *tondaru* instead of *tobikomu,* is known. Though rooted in the same verb *tobu* (to fly, jump, leap, vault, or flip) the two forms are quite different. In contrast to the rather straightforward *tobikomu, tondaru* suggests that something "has flipped" and, as a glide or contracted form of *tobitaru,* has an effect similar to saying "isn't" instead of "is not." For this reason, some think that Bashō composed the *tondaru* version while still an adherent of the Danrin school. There may have been an error in transcription or tampering by a wishful Danrin editor. But if Bashō did use the word in the first version and revised it to *tobikomu,* the change may have marked the conscious departure for his own school, the Shōfū.

Finally, the hokku has a wakiku, attributed to Kikaku. Whether there were other parts is unknown. The hokku and the wakiku together read:

Furuike ya kawazu tobikomu mizu no oto   Bashō
An old pond: a frog jumps in—the sound of water

  ashi no wakaba ni kakaru kumo no su   Kikaku
  suspended over young rush blades, a spider's web

There are several references to the hokku by Bashō's contemporaries. Those by Kyorai and Tohō have already been quoted. The only other notable reference is that by Shikō in his *Kuzu no Matsubara* (Pine Grove with Kudzu), published in 1692. It tells how Bashō one day came up with the seven- and five-syllable lines first, rejected the phrase *yamabuki ya* (kerria rose) that Kikaku suggested for the first five, and settled on his own *furuike ya.* The story is considered reliable, but some have pointed out that for it to be believed the date of the composition of the hokku must be pushed back to 1681 or 1684. Yamamoto Kenkichi says either year would be acceptable for the *tondaru* version. In 1868 Kitsuda Shunko (1815–86) published *Bashō-ō Furuike Shinden* (A True History of the Venerable Bashō's Old Pond), which he said was his transcript of an old text found in the province of Mikawa. An obvious amplification of Shikō's story and a clumsy attempt to read Zen import into the hokku, the *Shinden* is now thought to be a hoax. It does, however, indicate how far the indigenous Zen interpretation of the hokku had gone by the end of the Edo period.

The compilation that follows is grouped into two sections. The first section is the result so far of what I initially set out to make: a collection of English translations of Bashō's hokku on an old pond. It is chronologically arranged and covers the period from the end of the nineteenth century to 1981. When the initial collection was ready, I sent it to my friends and asked for their own translations and variations. The second section is a corpus of their responses. Most of it was published in *Chanoyu Quarterly*, no. 19 (1978). The arrangement here is alphabetical, by author.

The greatest contributor to the first section is Kondō Tadashi, whose collection of fifty-one for his master's degree William J. Higginson passed on to me along with his own addition of several. Ross Figgins, a Californian haiku bibliographer, sent in thirty. Both Mr. Higginson and Mr. Figgins were impeccable gentlemen in providing bibliographies, thereby rectifying my sloppiness in that direction. To them, and to those who responded graciously to my request for their own tries, I can only be a grateful frog. For some who might be interested in the import of the "sound," Eleanor Wolff pointed to Arthur Avalon's *Serpent Power* (Madras: Ganesh and Co. Private Ltd., 1957) and Robin Hough to various paragraphs of the *Upanishads*. As Mr. Hough says, our frog actually puts in his appearance in the twenty-second paragraph, titled in Robert Hume's translation, "Reaching the higher, non-sound Brahma by meditation on the sound 'Om' " of the *Maitri Upanishad* (Oxford: Oxford University Press, 1971). More recently, David Attenborough, in *Life on Earth* (Boston: Little, Brown and Company, 1981), has speculated that the first voice on this globe came from a frog—but that is another story.

I

MASAOKA SHIKI

The old mere!
A frog jumping in
The sound of water

LAFCADIO HEARN

Old pond—frogs jumped in—sound of water.

W. G. ASTON

An ancient pond!
With a sound from the water
Of the frog as it plunges in.

BASIL HALL CHAMBERLAIN

The old pond, aye! and the sound of a frog leaping into the
water.

CLARA A. WALSH

An old-time pond, from off whose shadowed depth
Is heard the splash where some lithe frog leaps in.

WILLIAM J. PORTER

Stillness

Into the calm old lake
A frog with flying leap goes plop!
The peaceful hush to break.

GERTRUDE EMERSON

Old pond, aye! and the sound of a frog jumping in.

YONE NOGUCHI

The old pond!
A frog leapt into—
List, the water sound!

CURTIS HIDDEN PAGE

A lonely pond in age-old stillness sleeps . . .
    Apart, unstirred by sound or motion . . . till
Suddenly into it a lithe frog leaps.

INAZO NITOBE

Into an old pond
A frog took a sudden plunge,
Then is heard a splash.

JOHN THOMAS BRYAN

There is the old pond!
    Lo, into it jumps a frog:
hark, water's music!

ASATARO MIYAMORI

The old pond!
    A frog has plunged—
    The splash!

152 · TRANSLATING INTO ENGLISH

Into the calm old pond
A frog plunged—then the splash.

ASATARO MIYAMORI

The Old Pond

The ancient pond!
A frog plunged—splash!

The old pond! A frog plunged—
The sound of the water!

HIDESABURO SAITO

Old garden lake!
The frog thy depth doth seek,
And sleeping echoes wake.

MINORU TOYODA

An ancient pond!
A frog leaps in;
The sound of the water!

HAROLD G. HENDERSON

An ancient pond;
Plash of the water
When a frog jumps in.

FUMIKO SAISHO

Fu-ru (old) *i-ke* (pond) *ya, ka-wa-zu* (frog) *to-bi-ko-mu*
(jumping into) *mi-zu* (water) *no o-to* (sound)

INAZO NITOBE

An old pond—
A frog jumps in—
A splash of water.

DAISETZ T. SUZUKI

Into the ancient pond
A frog jumps
Water's sound!

R. H. BLYTH

The old pond.
A frog jumps in—
Plop!

KENNETH YASUDA

Ancient pond unstirred
Into which a frog has plunged,
A splash was heard.

R. H. BLYTH

The old pond;
A frog jumps in,—
The sound of the water.

G. S. FRASER

The old pond, yes!
A frog jumping in.
The water's noise!

The old pond, yes, and
A frog-jumping-in-the-
Water's noise!

Old pond, yes, and
Frog-jump-in-
Water's noise.

Old pond, yes, and
Frog jump in!
Water's noise!

DONALD KEENE

The ancient pond
A frog leaps in
The sound of the water.

The ancient pond, a frog jumps in, the sound of the water.

KENNETH REXROTH

An old pond—
The sound
Of a diving frog.

PETER BEILENSON

OLD DARK SLEEPY POOL . . .
QUICK UNEXPECTED
FROG
GOES PLOP! WATERSPLASH!

HAROLD G. HENDERSON

Old pond:
   frog jump-in
      water-sound.

Old-pond : frog jump-in : water-sound

Old pond—
   and a frog-jump-in
      water-sound

NIPPON GAKUJUTSU SHINKŌKAI
(an institution)

The old pond!
A frog jumps in—
Sound of the water.

HIROSHI TAKAMINE

Oh, into the old pond
   A frog plunged,
      With a splash!
         (And once again calm prevails!)

ANONYMOUS (as cited in the *Times Literary Supplement*)

Ancient pond;
   frog jumps in;
      sound of water.

CID CORMAN

old pond
frog leaping
splash

DAISETZ T. SUZUKI

The old pond, ah!
A frog jumps in:
The water's sound.

HAROLD STEWART

The old green pond is silent; here the hop
Of a frog plumbs the evening stillness: plop!

SHUNKICHI AKIMOTO

Into the old pond
Leaps a frog
Lo, the sound of the water.

PETER BEILENSON and HARRY BEHN

AN OLD SILENT POND . . .
INTO THE POND
A FROG JUMPS,
SPLASH! SILENCE AGAIN.

EDWARD G. SEIDENSTICKER

The quiet pond
A frog leaps in,
The sound of the water.

DION O'DONNOL

AYE, THE OLD POND AND
A-FROG-THAT-IS-A-LEAPING-IN-THE-WATER

HARRY BEHN

An old silent pond . . .
A frog jumps into the pond,
splash! Silence again.

GEOFFREY BOWNAS and ANTHONY THWAITE

An old pond
A frog jumps in—
Sound of water.

MASARU V. OTAKE

The old pond,
Frog jumps in—
The sound of water.

NOBUYUKI YUASA

Breaking the silence
Of an ancient pond,
A frog jumped into water—
A deep resonance.

SCOTT ALEXANDER

By an ancient pond
a bullfrog sits on a rock
waiting for Basho?

SYLVIA CASSEDY and KUNIHIRO SUETAKE

Old pond, blackly still—
frog, plunging into water,
splinters silent air.

Old pond:
frog jump in
water-sound.

DION O'DONNOL

The silent old pond
a mirror of ancient calm,
a frog-leaps-in splash . . .

ANONYMOUS (as cited in *Don't Tell the Scarecrow*)

The old pond.
A frog jumps into the water—
SPLASH.

EDWARD BOND

> Silent old pool
> Frog jumps
> Kdang!

CANA MAEDA

> old pond
>   a frog in-leaping
>   water-note

G. S. FRASER

> The old pond, yes, and
> A frog is jumping into
> The water, and splash.

> Old pond, yes, and
> Frog jumping into
> The water's noise.

> Old pond, yes,
> Frog there jumping,
> Water's noise.

ARMANDO MARTINS JANEIRA

> Ah, the old pond
> A frog jumps in
> Sound of water.

MAKOTO UEDA

> The old pond—
> A frog leaps in,
> And a splash.

WILLIAM J. HIGGINSON

Old pond . . .
 a frog leaps in
  water's sound.

ROBERT H. BROWER

The ancient pond:
A frog jumps in—
The sound of water.

WILLIAM HOWARD COHEN

Mossy pond;
frog leaping in—
splash!

KENJUN IKEDA

The old pond!
A frog jumps in
With splash-splosh.

DANIEL C. BUCHANAN

Into the old pond
A frog suddenly plunges.
The sound of water.

DOROTHY BRITTON

Listen! a frog
 Jumping into the stillness
  Of an ancient pond!

JOAN GIROUX

An old pond
A frog jumps in
The sound of the water.

ALFRED H. MARKS

The old pond:
A frog jumps in,—
The sound of the water

(limerick)

There once was a curious frog
Who sat by a pond on a log
And, to see what resulted,
In the pond catapulted
With a water-noise heard round the bog.

(sonnet)

A frog who would a-water-sounding go
Into some obscure algae-covered pool
Had best be sure no poetasting fool
Is waiting in the weeds and, to his woe,
Commemorates his pluck so all will know
His name and lineage, not for the fine school
He learned to sing at, nor, to make men drool
The flavor of his leg from thigh to toe.
He will not for his mother be remembered,
Nor for his father's deeds, his honor bright,
Nor for his brother's leg dismembered,
And eaten by a king with rare delight.
He will be famous simply for the sorta
Noise he makes just when he hits the water.

Basho

Swoop!
Green, bug-eyed, wingless, conquering air,
earth-thrusting legs outstretched in triumph;
descending,
striking,
submerging in jade, groundless depths.
And above
the jet thrown high tumbles,
the shaken air composes to silence;
the rings of water spread, strike shore,
return colliding and subside.

ROBERT AITKEN

Old   pond   ! / Frog   jumps in / Water   's sound

The old pond;
A frog jumps in,—
The sound of the water.

The old pond has no walls.
The frog simply jumped in,
And his sound does not echo at all.

FELIX-MARTI IBANEZ

The old pond!
A frog jumps:
Sound of water!

LUCIEN STRYK and TAKASHI IKEMOTO

Old pond,
leap-splash—
a frog.

ROBERT AITKEN

> The old pond;
> A frog jumps in—
> The sound of the water.

(word-for-word)

> Old pond!
> frog jumps in
> water of sound

> The old pond has no walls;
> A frog just jumps in;
> Do you say there is an echo?

EARL MINER

> The still old pond
> and as a frog leaps in it
> the sound of a splash

ALLEN GINSBERG

> The old pond
> A frog jumped in,
> Kerplunk!

EARL MINER and HIROKO ODAGIRI

> The old pond is still
> a frog leaps right into it
> splashing the water

YOKO DANNO

> Old-pond—a frog
> leaps in
> water sound

BILL DEEMER

HIGH KUKU

> I enlightened Bashō,
> recalled the Frog,
> but he scared me!

BERNARD LIONEL EINBOND

> Antic pond—
> frantic frog jumps in—
> gigantic sound.

> Into an old pond,
> a leaping frog tumbles—
> the sound of water.

> An old pond—
> a frog tumbles in—
> the water's sound.

> from "Insomnia in Haiku Form"
>
> 16
>
> Unable to sleep—
> I imagine an old pond,
> and a frog jumps in.

ROBERT ANTHONY FAGAN

from "Travels"

hey
the frog's fallen
in the pond
splash

ROSS FIGGINS

Some Notes on the Old Pond

1. After working with this for a while, I can't resist a pun.
   I don't know the legitimacy of word plays in translations,
   but . . .

   > old pond,
   >   frog jump in—
   >   a sound question

2. The next is an attempt to capture the sound by bracketing
   it between the interrupted moments of silence. The ambi-
   guity is intended.

   > old pond,
   >   a frog leaps in—
   >   a moment after, silence

3. And finally a more literal interpretation.

   > old pond—
   >   the sound
   >   of a frog and water

transliteration

. . . old . . pond . . .
. . . frog . leap . . .
. . . water sound . . .

transvisions

stillness . . .
a frog-pond ploomp!
makes it breathe,

the universe . . .	ab-sence	(samsara)
a froglet moves it	bare attention	(satipatthana)
listen!	presence	(nirvana)

silent mystery . .	dead pond
a tiny frog	tiny frog
sounds its depths.	live mind

the wordless Word:	nay
a frog-pond plop	yea
makes it heard.	aye
	?
	!
	.

bearded pond,
tickled by frog,
says, "ugh!" . . . & smiles.

my mind was still
till Bashō's frog
made it ripple.

                              pond plus frog is what?:
                              splash? plash? or plop?
                              ploop? ploomp? or flop?

LORRAINE ELLIS HARR

    The quiet pond;
    And a frog jumps
    Splash!

                    The old pond:
                      A frog jumps into it—
                              Plip/plop

                    Quiet pond:
                              Frog-jump-in
                                      Plop-sound.

                    A quiet pond;
                      A frog jumps
                              kersplat!

                    Blip!
                        A frog plunges
                                into the pond.

                    Mossy pond:
                      Plunging frog's
                              water-blip.

                    Quiet old pool:
                                      Blip!
                    a frog jumps-in.

Water-gluck:
Into the old pond
    a frog jumps

Old mossy pond;
a frog jumps
        blip/splat

Blip/splat!
Into the old mossy pond
    a frog jumps—

LINDLEY WILLIAMS HUBBELL

I've made two tries:

An old pond
A frog jumping
Sound of water

but after reading Curtis Hidden Page I felt that my version
was terribly unpoetical, so I tried again:

Oh thou unrippled pool of quietness
Upon whose shimmering surface, like the tears
Of olden days, a small batrachian leaps,
The while aquatic sounds assail our ears.

HISAO KANASEKI

an old pond:
noises of frogs
leaping in

JAMES KIRKUP

Age-old pond stillness.
Jump of a frog disturbs it
With a little plop.

pond
    frog
        plop!

FRANK KUENSTLER

from *EMPIRE*

Once upon a time there was a frog
Once upon a time there was a pond
Splash.

WILLIAM MATHESON

from "Ten Variations on Bashō's 'Pond and Frog' *Haiku*"

   III

Jumpe, jumpe, lyttle Frogge!
Water soundeth
All aroundeth
In thyss olde Bogge.

   VIII

——ah vecchio stagno——
——una rana ha saltato
   . . . dell'acqua il suono . . .

X

"And what, after all," she paused, as if taking advantage—which he knew (oh, yes! he knew) she *was,* by heaven!, doing—of the last of the October light so parsimoniously, and yet with such prodigality, such largesse, being filtered into the room through the window giving on to the Park (but such squalid little panes! he could not help himself—and considering every-thing, considering particularly *this* thing, why *should* he help himself—from thinking), "did, as you seemingly want to tell me about it, 'happen,'—I believe that was how you expressed it?"

"Well," he began, with every intention of holding it up, confound it!; it was now, or, to coin a phrase, never.

"Well'?" she held fire and there it was, in all its shabby, its commercial, glory, glittering and luminous, between them. "Only 'well'?"

"Well," taking a perverse delight in the slowness of his enunciation, as how often, God only knows, these last months, *she* had and over matters infinitely less, to her but unfortunately not to him, important, "there was a noise, a sound, an echo, one might say."

"One 'might,' but should one, should particularly *you,* say so?"

"Oh, well, I, for all that. . . ." She sailed beyond his modest disclaimer, as she always managed, somehow, and in spite of what were to her, at least, genuine feelings of respect—if that was what he wanted—for him, to do. "And," she continued, she so invincibly continued, contriving in some fashion, out of some font of charity, some well-spring of *tendresse,* to give him, if not breathing-space, at least time to take a turn around the, he thought, wretched little *chambre de bonne* which she had the pretension to call—and the miracle of it was, had had the force, or merely the cleverness, of character to cause others to call—a "salon," "this 'noise,' this 'sound,' what exactly, if you'll allow me the indiscretion, *was* it? What, if I may be so bold to ask, *made* it?"

"Ah, as to the making of it, and I think it charming, *en dernière analyse,* for you to use the word, when all is said and done," knowing, as he full well *did* know, that nothing, indeed, had been said or done, that nearly nothing had even begun being "said" and that, there being worlds still to be said, surely nothing could even be considered as being "done," "that's a relatively simple matter: it jumped, or leapt, or threw itself, or was propelled—*le choix est à vous*—into it, and consequently, as such is often the case, it made a noise."

"I hope you don't, after all these years, find me—it would be shocking, my love, if you *did,* but these things happen— benighted or unenlightened, or simply deficient, but," her fine (as fine as in Florence) eyes searched vaguely for his, as though this were the last of her beacons, the last of all harbors in which to anchor her craft, "if you'll permit me, what 'jumped' into what and what made what 'noise'?"

"Ah, *there,* my dear, you have it, *all* of it. Or, rather, wouldn't you say?, we *both* have it, all of it, in all its little quivering, tremulous, so preciously ephemeral, being?"

"I cannot say, precisely, that *I* have it, but I am comforted, if that is the word, by *your* having it, having it so utterly yours, as you have always had," her face in the nearly posthumous effulgence of twilight turning slowly, and as if for the last, the desperately last, time, from his, "everything."

R. CLARENCE MATSUO-ALLARD

ancient pond—
  a frog jumping into its splash

CLARE NIKT

Hear the lively song
of the frog in
BrrrBrrrBrrrptyBrrrBrrrrrrrrrrIp.
Plash!

MICHAEL O'BRIEN

My Noble Lord:
The cat just pissed on the Basho translations.
O ancient lake!

MAUREEN OWEN

The Origin of Haiku

for Bashō

The little frog   lost his footing

RON PADGETT

"Advertising translation"

old pond
frog jumps in
plop plop fizz fizz

CYRIL PATTERSON

Without pondering its next leap,
a bullfrog makes its splash!

The spirit
of the old pond is
frog-bound.

```
A        a
pon      fat
der      old
ous      frog
oc       goes
ca
sion     plop!
```

Finality—
a bullfrog croaks beside
the lily pond.

Zen leap—
a bullfrog makes its
splash!

Without pondering
its next leap,
a bullfrog makes its
splash!

One frog flattened
on the road—
another croaks beside
the lily pond.

From the pond's edge,
a bullfrog PLOPS into
oblivion.

BARBARA RUCH

An old green pond.
A small green frog dives in.
The ping of water.

ELEANOR WOLFF

Age-old pool ya
A frog jumps into
the water: the sound of it

Old old pond ya
Sound, as a frog jumps in,
of water . . . .

GEORGE M. YOUNG, JR.

After perusing *Basho's Furuike,* I checked, and sure enough
found in my file of yellowed newspaper clippings the following
notice:

MAFIA HIT-MAN POET: NOTE FOUND PINNED TO LAPEL OF
DROWNED VICTIM'S DOUBLE-BREASTED SUIT! ! ! ! !

> Dere wasa dis frogg
> Gone jumpa offa da logg
> Now he inna bogg.
> —Anonymous

According to the newspaper account, neither the author's
nor the victim's identity has yet been ascertained.

Thought you might be interested in this strange item—another
wrinkle to the age-old mystery of the frog and the pond.

PART THREE
COMPOSING IN ENGLISH

CHAPTER EIGHT

English Renga

Renga writing in the United States seems to have taken root in the middle of the 1970s. In 1975 *The End (& Variations Thereof)* printed a few English-language renga. The next year the Haiku Society of America held sessions on the form and published the traditional kasen format in its newsletter. This was followed by a special issue of *Haiku Magazine* with articles on the form and several renga sequences. Since then a number of renga have been published here and in Canada—first chiefly in *Cicada,* a magazine of the Haiku Society of Canada, and more recently in *Frogpond* of the Haiku Society of America. In announcing the stress to be put on renga, the editor of *Frogpond* said: "Linked poetry offers the possibility of poetry as conversation, or as group improvisation, rather than exhortation or lonely meditation. This in turn opens up refreshingly different roles for the poet, as participant rather than as alienated solipsist."

Although the English renga sequences I have seen are still not many, I may venture the following observations:

RULES   The rules followed seem in most cases limited to the minimum requirements of "disjunctive linking" and alternation of three-line and two-line parts (or long and short one-line parts). This should probably be continued, except perhaps that a few parts might mention a specific object to create points to return to. What that object should be is difficult to determine, and the object may vary from one sequence to another. Also, a general, if not strict, agreement might be made that repetition of the same or similar word or image be avoided within several consecutive parts.

FORMAT   The small size of each part should also be kept as it is. *Renga: A Chain of Poems,* the celebrated attempt published in 1972 by Octavio Paz, Jacques Roubaud, Eduardo Sanguineti, and Charles Tomlinson, seems to fail largely because each part is a sonnet; too much tends to be said in fourteen lines for the next link to follow up on and to give a conclusion to. The Kai group of Japanese poets (see page 112) seems to have discovered this quickly.

TIME AND MEANS   Most English renga are composed through correspondence and take up to a year to complete, in sharp contrast to Japanese attempts in which the effort is still made to complete a sequence in one sitting. The epistolary method probably should not be encouraged or discouraged, but the ample time this method allows for working on one's link may result in a series of sparklers. One of two things is recommended to avoid this: agree that one participant act as a coordinator willing to adjust his links according to the development of the sequence, or agree that participants hold back the urge to show off in every part.

The following selection is meant to give some idea of English renga now being written.

• Two-Part Excerpts •

from BLAZING TIDEFLATS: A SOLO RENGA
by Cor van den Heuvel

> the pigeons all rise at once
> and disappear around the corner

> in front of the bank—
> wondering where the money
> went

~

> the candles glow softly—
> blackout in New York City

> moonlight—
> a great liner, all lit up,
> heads out to sea

from THE SPLIT MOON
by William J. Higginson, Michael McClintock, and Elizabeth
Searle Lamb

> the pup whines
> quietly, tongue frozen
> to the axe-blade   Higginson

> the whiteness of it:
> this first snowdrop   Lamb

~

> the arguing diminishes
> to a small point out in the wind   McClintock

> a blue balloon
> escaping the five fingers
> lifts   Lamb

from A LATE BLIZZARD
by Elizabeth Searle Lamb, L. A. Davidson, and Virginia Brady
  Young

   stirred by the cold poker,
   pitch pine splits into flame   Davidson

   the old virgin
     walking on ice
   to her wedding . . .   Young

~

   with the twilight chill,
   she hugs her braless bosom   Young

   one mosquito . . .
     the moon rising
   into a cloud   Lamb

from OLD WOMAN'S BANJO: A ONE-LINE RENGA
by Marlene Wills, Elizabeth Searle Lamb, and Bill Pauly

   coffee cold in the waiting room   she awakens first   Wills

   another ambulance wails in   Lamb

~

   run of apple butter   the old reflection in her eyes   Wills

   the rocking chair rocking itself   Lamb

from JESUS LEAVING VEGAS
by Virginia Brady Young, Michael McClintock, and S. L. Poulter

   a bad day:
   the old woman's
             capillaries
   pucker   Young

   half a sandwich
   to eat slowly
   again tonight   McClintock

~

cracking
out of the wind
the sound of leaves   Poulter

something light
as thistles . . .
the last birdsong   Young

                              ~

smoothing his rags,
  the hobo enters
      the deserted house   Young

radio static . . .
rain
on a window   McClintock

from LINKED POEM
by William Matheson, Kyoko Selden, and Hiroaki Sato

all mechanized
and artificialized, wild
soil won't recover   Sato

    "one must bear in mind one thing"
              thing what
      but what   thing
              thing what   Matheson

from THE RAGGED MISTS RENGA
by John Wills, Cor van den Heuvel, and Michael McClintock
(author not identified each time)

twenty TV screens glow
in the christmas tree ornament

the doll's house . . .
onto the crooked step
drops a pine needle

                              ~

beyond the doorway:
blood-spattered legs
in the glare of a flashbulb

incense . . . the ash tip
                            falls off

~

morning sunlight drifts down
from the wooded cliffs

piled on the beach
the crabs
grip one another

from LIN KED POEM
by James Kirkup, Hiroaki Sato, and Kyoko Selden

You cry; in this warm darkness
I do not know why you cry   Sato

The tree peonies
glow like lanterns in the dusk
of the melting year   Kirkup

~

under pale street lamps
dark pools flicker with dawn rains:
I am lost again.   Kirkup

Today streaks of fog tarry
over the Susquehanna.   Selden

from AUTUMN INSECTS
Solo Renga by Kyoko Selden

    closed eyes scan small print, pages
    of failures, unread letters

you've never seen your
face   mirror image has
right and left reversed

               ~

she awaits her death
she watches others await
her final waning

    what silk-thin difference is there
    if I stay to dream or go

from PEDALING A BIKE
by Tadashi Kondo, Philip Meredith, Kristine Young, Jody
   Rashburn, and Sakura Onishi

   the glare of the sun
   at the top of the mountain   Meredith

   eyes closed
   the warmth of tea
   seeps through the fingers   Young

               ~

   the bus sweeps past
   branches tapping windows
   bouncing grandmothers   Meredith

   giggling and chatting
   they rewrap their lunchboxes   Young

from Outside the Window
by Marlene Wills and Hiroaki Sato

   autumn evening after splitting wood his wedge   Wills

     divorce agreed upon, the house still shared   Sato

       ~

   the egg has feathers the chicken three legs   Sato

   how many zen monks to screw in a light bulb   Wills

from In Winter Rain
by Marlene Wills and Hiroaki Sato

     we shared a bed, bodies separate   Sato

   a dream from fifteen years mother chasing me through cor-
     ridors   Wills

       ~

   memories are close now that you are distant   Sato

   clouds drift your blue sock under the bed   Wills

from Linked Poem
by Michael O'Brien, William Matheson, Kyoko Selden, and
   Hiroaki Sato (author not identified each time)

   branch and grain of wood
   fish deceived and gulls beguiled
   are there tears for things

     the coat someone threw out
     is an old lady going through the garbage

       ~

did I hear cracked ice slither
did I see ice at water's edge
                              melt

melted by the whiskey
twists to the bottom, like smoke
like pale gold brocade

from LINKED POEM
by Kyoko Selden, William Matheson, and Hiroaki Sato

    where Cydonian quinces
    are fragrant in green lightning   Selden

where? at the clavier
Scarlatti fugue Tartini
ambiguities   Matheson

             ~

    not barking dogs: westering
    geese with their torch-bearing cry   Matheson

dead woman's spirit
heard weaving at the bottom
of winter water   Selden

from OPIUM
by Geoffrey O'Brien, Michael O'Brien, and Hiroaki Sato
(author not identified each time)

each scattered
flower's a planet,
whirling detached

    corolla of ego, habit, circumstance
    "no-one's sleep under so many eyelids"

           ~

massed and lonely,
a migration
a moving wall

   the woodchuck shows enough sense
   to run from the camera's click

~

breeze stirring the curtains
of so many rooms,
the late, empty light

   as she rolls the blind down:
   crescent leaning toward water tower

• Full Sequences •

BRONZE SHIELD
by Geoffrey O'Brien, Hiroaki Sato, and James Kirkup
New York City, London, Kyoto
from February 1980 to January 1981

bronze shield, by mezzo-
tint of picnic girls. steady rain
chills the museum   O'Brien

    my girlfriend comes fully dressed
    suffering from monilia   Sato

on the nord express
the diva next door practising
Isolde all night long   Kirkup

    past thickets, benches, the river
    tumbles forward in spring flood   O'Brien

in my dream, mother's
left eye now gelatinous,
mouth agape with grief   Sato

    nostrils listen, ears observe—
    eyes feel, numb with enlightenment   Kirkup

pieces of face toss
in air as the mirror hits
the floor. the sky stays calm   O'Brien

    after a hint of pain
    we walk to a Turkish bath   Sato

and the next moment
the rainy season started
with a banging door   Kirkup

    the street humid and empty
    "you wanna buy a radio?"   O'Brien

ENGLISH RENGA · *189*

"wanna be my friend?"
the voice, its echo, down those
streets, through these years   Sato

    loudspeaker summer's campaigns—
    blood, sweat and electioneers   Kirkup

by midtown airshaft,
only the shrill whirring
of a giant fan   O'Brien

    someone's wife is someone's wife,
    face buried in someone's chest   Sato

I dreamed of our Queen
wearing harlequin glasses
with the Crown of State   Kirkup

    waking, eyes still ache from the
    wide bright plain I got lost in   O'Brien

a Navaho boy
one with a crawling donkey
the only dark spot   Sato

    afterimage—your green grace
    bright as a red ghost at noon   Kirkup

Goethe yelled: "More light!"
I trust my last words may be:
"My! Whatever next?"   Kirkup

    Bashō on his death bed chose
    scattering over dustless   Sato

laying the book down,
trying to read the floppy
non-denoting leaves   O'Brien

    on my walkman set, listen
    to my own voice's poems   Kirkup

''She didn't suffer
'cause she heard only herself,
but one never knows''   Sato

   ''Please don't go''—girl I've not met
   bangs on the wall one floor up   O'Brien

the street's reflections
throw themselves out of windows
opened with a scream   Kirkup

   mother breathes drip by drip,
   Marilyn Chambers perspires   Sato

summer goes: as I
sprawl by the fire escape,
the first cool breeze   O'Brien

   a dead leaf shifts sideways—no!
   it's a little tinted crab   Kirkup

another movement,
but this time with all the right
tones behind it   Sato

   within the sustained note
   echoes echo themselves   O'Brien

and in my next life
this temple bell is ringing
before it is struck   Kirkup

   through flu-flattened afternoon
   phone goes on and on and on   Sato

''I heard the shots, I
thought it was a truck backfiring—
I mean, I knew it wasn't''   O'Brien

   deep snow   silence   loneliness—
   we want to hold your hand   Kirkup

trees are all in flower
but this avocado mayn't leaf
unfleshed before Christmas   Sato

   in the sudden brilliant cold
   the messenger's milky eyes   O'Brien

RICKSHAW (OR BUDDHA COMES TO THE WEST)
Solo Renga by Cor van den Heuvel
New York City
Winter 1979–80

summer rain—
a rickshaw climbs a hill
in an old movie

Peter Lorre, wearing a white suit,
comes through the beaded curtain

under a ceiling fan,
the chair turns slowly around
with Sidney Greenstreet

the marquee lights whirl
in the gloss of her lipstick

bursting from the squad car
the cop runs toward the bar
his neon badge pulsing

the highway veers off into darkness
in both directions

clearing sky—
the hiker unfolds
the milky way

the trail map indicates
a steep climb to the peak

reflections
grow still in the dawn lake—
om mani padme hum

slowly disappearing on the ledge—
the lapping marks above the waterline

the afternoon sun brightens
everything: the blue sky, the woods,
even the shadows

an ant comes out of the hole
drops a grain of sand and goes back in

she stops
on the secluded path
to look at her engagement ring

along the frozen river,
the cliffs are encased in ice

stained with dogs' pee,
the old snowman watches
the moon rise

the beautiful mannequin
gazes through reflections

fluttering wings
leave a streak of colored dust
on the girl's finger

reading a haiku by Buson
about a caterpillar's hairs

a wind comes off the ocean
shaking all the car antennas
in the parking lot

spray flies from the shadowed waves
into the rays of the setting sun

darkness is gaining—
on deck, a lone man points
into the distance

As the fog thickens
by Hiroaki Sato, Geraldine Little, and Marlene Wills
New York, New Jersey, and Tennessee
from October 1980 to June 1981

As the fog thickens
the mother goes on reading,
her two children playing in the waves   Sato

over the sand castle,
blue voices of gulls   Little

that song again of bessie's
a neighbor wants to buy
the dying elm   Wills

eating noodles & thinking
"Let me weep for once"   Sato

on the table
the candle sputters out—
who's playing Bach   Little

alone late night breath
ing of the wood stove   Wills

is this glow of love
I feel when separated
a false sentiment   Sato

the songs of waking birds
and wind through leafless trees   Little

the short day
letting the cat out
letting the cat in   Wills

and he: "in and out
and back to work"   Sato

in the bath her limbs
under rippled reflections:
ashes on the hearth   Little

    heart to heart talk
    and a self portrait   Wills

in the dark, eyes closed,
your face resembles that of
the Lord Buddha   Sato

    thinking of the moon
    when it is full on the fields   Little

reeds frozen
after smoking
our oralness   Wills

    cough, then the sound of a shower
    from the neighbor downstairs   Sato

watching steam
from the teakettle
sketch clouds   Little

    mountain in haze
    behind a billboard   Wills

when my heart is reposed
hers trembles with pain,
and vice versa   Sato

    I think back to that morning
    we shared an old toothbrush   Wills

opening blinds
the rush of sun, the crystal vase
suddenly full   Little

    let's imagine icicles
    on that house-shaped bird feeder   Sato

it would have made sense
the speeding ticket getting home
rather than to work   Wills

   across the driveway
   the musky smell of moonrise   Little

a mansion like this
I haven't seen for long
and that has made me drunk   Sato

   new strings on the banjo
   up late listening for a song   Wills

an owl tuning up
the twelve-tone scale of neighbors
quarreling again   Little

   the cause and the end may be
   a simple interruption   Sato

on our minds now
manure and seeds
and signs in the breasts   Wills

   even the old cracked mirror
   reflects blended images   Little

déjà vu:
finding oneself in a position
one was once seen in   Sato

   our love will it too fade
   (like grass under a fallen stone)   Wills

an old couple
ponders a fossil—twisted blades
of a spent summer   Little

   "You don't seem to understand"
   "No, look at it from this side"   Sato

no phone calls
nothing in the mail
the full moon   Wills

　on the terrace a clay urn
　brims: shine and blue shadows   Little

IN YOUR PANTIES
Solo Renga on Love by Hiroaki Sato
New York City
January and February 1982

Jilted and distracted this past winter, I decided to write poems in renga form—the form best suited to someone who can't concentrate. Here is one of them:

In your panties
slightly pulled down
a crisp fallen leaf

    wetness a surprise
    to the initiate

tears flow
as fingers trace them
in warm darkness

    they sit up in the grass,
    look at the city they left

"You are that moon,
a face I've remembered
from another land"

    falling for someone
    who'd just had his turn

her firm shoulders
when hugged, stiffened,
and I didn't care

    "I won't let you go"
    can't be shaken off

he stares out
at lit windows, lit towers,
beyond her head

nose still moist with
the smell of sex

hunger afterward
then to an eatery
a cavern

elegant lovers dining
a photo for an ad

for this tryst
underwear selected
negligently

she waits under the moon
for a third in three nights

how enlightening
the phrase was when first heard:
"sex-starved"

in love nothing changes
and everything does

like cherry flowers
in distant haze, you glow
but not for me

who will be the next
to hear you moan and coo?

"I didn't mean to . . ."
"If you meant to, you've
succeeded"

the awaited word
and aimless release

the day breaks,
he walks off fully dressed
under her gaze

    working out an alba
    getting a taxi

four hours or four
seconds sex lasts only
while it lasts

    pleasure of reading
    of those who love love

every morning
at Fiftieth and Eighth
I pass a woman

    she looks away or up
    I look ahead or down

a third entry
makes gentleness jar
smiles bruise

    long wedded to his habits
    he thinks of one thing

"I was more struck
than charmed, yes, by your homage
to the moon"

    thought from the past confessed
    after snifters of Jack Daniel's

these people here
mayn't after all be all
for hitting the sheets

    loneliness forgotten
    midnight, in city snow

below us
white flakes in the lamplight
rising aslant

    you two almost make love
    in public, I've been told

"Here are flowers
to make up for my
petty protests"

    two dandelions between
    your outstretched thighs

PAST MIDSUMMER
by Michael O'Brien, Lindley Williams Hubbell, and Hiroaki
   Sato
New York City, Kamikōshien, Santa Fe
from July 1979 to March 1980
(author not identified each time)

Past midsummer, but
the year's arrested fall still
papers a late wall with light.

   The rainy season is over in Kyushu,
   but my windows are still blurred.

Only when I'm drunk
or the demon's away, I say what's
never forgotten.

   A tangle of saplings behind the house
   on the way to the mailbox.

Letters from three continents
in today's mail.
I rest in the center.

   After twelve years of mud-spewing
   I neither hate nor love you.

O careless love,
alone in the music,
the band alone in the music.

   Love comes to us
   when we can live without it.

In the southwest
trees grow
where there is a river.

   The eye is a horse
   which drinks and drinks.

Insatiably
my eyes drink:
animal, vegetable, mineral.

    Constance Money, Annette Haven,
    and Anna Obsessed

the iconostasis before the mystery,
smoke rising in the projector's beam
from a rapt audience

    icons drifting by . . .
    Mary Pickford . . . Linda Lovelace

and while on the subject
I have everything
and nothing to say

    an old junkie
    turning the pages

for seventy years
I have been turning the pages
of the same books

    generations of sparrows
    have pecked those holes on that brick wall

and the eye pivots
from page to wall
checking the manifest

    two mature angels in relief
    hold a scroll painting

Sappho rises
from the graves of Oxyrhynchus
like new moons of Saturn

    Lethe, honeycomb, wide missouri
    o pearl-handed dawn

I remember
walking home along buildings,
another night ended

  all night at Nara
  the crying of the deer

"that now are wild"
in careless love
down by the river

  rustling the leaves you were an adult,
  I was a novice

rain falls quietly
on the belated celebrants
O tu Palermo

  nothing intact as memory
  no dawn so clear

on the subway:
"It won't do until you forget it."
"But I won't."

  a miner is not qualified
  to appraise gems

finders, not keepers
of the adornments
of their dark throat of earth

  of gold
  that stretches the thinnest

Agamemnon's body
disappeared into dust
before their eyes

  sun-shot king-work
  unravelling in air

Japanese are to rebuild
the Tower of Babel
where the rivers shift

let us honor
the birthplace of language

~·~ CHAPTER NINE ~·~

English Haiku

American haiku poets, living in a tradition that emphasizes freedom rather than conformity, show a distinct "willingness to experiment with ever new forms," as Alfred Marks put it in his essay on "Haiku in Japanese and English" (*Chanoyu Quarterly*, no. 9, 1974). Although there are still many who count syllables and put them in three neat lines aligned at left, many others cast their haiku in an extensive variety of typographical formations, while some compose delightful concrete haiku, so to speak. It is, indeed, no longer flippant to say "a haiku is what is so designated by its author." In view of this situation the Haiku Society of America, when sponsoring contests for high school students in 1979 and 1980, defined the haiku as "a poem in three lines or less," such as:

sunset on the pond—
the edge of the ice sharpens
    into dark water   Clyde C. Glandon

morning snow falls
  smoke rises   Stephen Wolfe

pig and I spring rain   Marlene Wills

The following selection is meant to give a glimpse of haiku now being written in the United States.

Up the gusty street,
  an umbrella, belly front,
    bobbing on two feet.

white cloud scudding
across a blue sky
GULL'S
the cry

where sea and sky meet
only hazy fishing boats
  dividing the gray

The seagull
bashing it against the rock
    one more time.

using the time
washing his teeth on deck
to view the moon

wind changing
with the shape of sandstone
changing with the wind

an old farmstead
bought for investment;
the wild columbine

a few old people
on steps of the gray church,
the bell still ringing

winter morning
without leaf or flower
the shape of the tree

the eye hospital;
from a snowy window ledge
the pigeon peering in

somewhere long ago
this black hawk in a bare tree,
the snow deep below

coming into it
from the bitter cold:
the warmth of her house

Haibun: *In the Peruvian Andes*

Cuzco. The city lies in a green valley nearly 12,000 feet above the Peruvian seacoast 300 miles to the west. Here, probably around AD 1200, Manco Capac founded his Inca Empire. Here, Francisco Pizarro in 1533 conquered in the name of Spain. And here, now, a provincial capital of Peru. The mix of cultures and remnants of cultures pulls the visitor into many levels of time.

church bells
and Cuzco's red tile roofs
in dawnmist

The air is thin. The sun burns hot when the sky is clear, but often the clouds gather and mist becomes a cold rain.

a street musician
shelters his harp with pink plastic
and goes on playing

a single coca leaf
in the frayed red coca bag
bought at the market

Inca stones are in the streets, in the buildings of Cuzco. And outside of the city, not far, are Inca ruins. Tambomachai or the Inca's Bath, Puca Pucara and Kenko. Even more ancient than these are the vast gray stones of the angled fortress wall, Sacsahuamán. Pre-Inca, says the guide.

the little Indian girl
herding her llamas
never stops spinning

Sunday is market day in the small Indian village of Pisac.

in the crumbling church
a little more dust filters down:
conch shell trumpets

hearing . . . not hearing
when Sunday mass is said
in Quechua!

as her mother kneels
a bright-eyed baby pulls at flowers
beside the saint's statue

Going by train through the Urubamba Valley toward Machu Picchu: blossoming orchids on rocks near the rapids, vine bamboo and flowering trees.

on the steep hillsides
up from the roaring Urubamba River
still . . . the old, old terraces

At last, after small buses climb the almost vertical side of the mountain by means of thirteen hairpin curves, the ruins of the Inca never found by the Spanish.

here at Machu Picchu
a begonia growing in the stone wall
and blossoming

dried alpaca dung
beside the sacred condor stone;
clouds cover the higher peaks

an ancient silence
in this plaza of the Inca—
but no! crickets

knitting—
> her needles ticking
> > in time to Mozart

Spring morning:
the dying calf's breath
moves into mist.

how the lake
> outer skin to roots, accommodates
> > the winter moon

The white spider
> whiter still
> > in the lightning's flash

out of the fog
> only the leap and fall
> > of a fish

The hole
where the shot bird was.
Snow falls and falls

thinking of crackling fires   your name   twisting down iced
> wind

miles of beach
and the winter stars
your hand in mine

on a snow-dusted twig remnant of robin song

RAYMOND ROSELIEP

Boy in a red cap

    s
     q
      u
       i
        r
         t
          i
           n
            g
             a
              y
               e
                l
                l
               o
              w
             a
            r
            c

on the very first snow

  with their pipes
hunched under spring sky
  old men make clouds

in the widow's veil
stars
blown from dandelion

but, child,
there is no song
in the egg you break

spring breeze
puffs through the skeleton
of a bird

blues are the big thing
with Monet, she said,
spreading the Roquefort

After Dusk

  asleep
the firefly
  is fueling

  sparks
however small
  light lovers

  our bodies
listen
  to light

the farmer talks corn,
pointing where the corn
is talking

my mother stock-still
before the balloon I put
on my father's grave

he removes his glove
      to point out
             Orion

trees unleaf;
my mother
grows smaller

walking in rain
I pass a stranger
    I know

rain
erasing
the clown's face

the snowflake disappears into its drop of water

the sun goes down—
my shovel strikes a spark
from the dark earth

spring mountains
in the doorknob
of the insane asylum

playing ball—
the girls
bounce

the shadow in the folded napkin

morning—
rain runs down
the drive-in movie screen

nothing
in the box—
the winter wind

cloudy day—
a branch of the tree
goes by the window forever

the moon rises—
dark shadows spread
under the cabbage plants

tidepool
in a clam shell—
the evening sunlight

hot night—
turning the pillow
to the cool side

Senryū

in her dressing room
the stripper powders her breasts—
and whispers something to them

the nude mannequin
in the dress-shop window
. . . looks away

ovulation fold of the mountain scattered with mist

old towel   folding it again   autumn evening

over my fingers
a stranger spills
the whiteness of night

cold outside
cold inside
warm ( )side

$$\begin{array}{cccc} 1 & & 1 & \\ a & a & a & a \\ b & b & b & b \\ i & i & i & i \\ u & u & u & u \\ & m & m & \end{array}$$

our triangle

pipes thaw   red spot on the egg yolk

first bleeding of the year

green appearing under cow hooves

pig and i spring rain

pushing hair behind my ears   spring woods

gosling following its neck to the bug

morning-glory folds into herself into her folds

one fly everywhere the heat

at dusk hot water from the hose

leaving him she whispered in the grocery store

after your visit
middle of the closet
empty hangers

autumn night   the phone rings twice and stops

```
        o       g
     r
f                frog
```

```
              rain
              dr p
               o
```

```
  k k k k
c c c c c c c
o o o o o o o
c c c c c c c
  a a a a a
    e e e
      p


                  o
          m           n
                  o
              _____
                  m
                  o
                  o
                  n
```

220 · COMPOSING IN ENGLISH

VIRGINIA BRADY YOUNG

During a downpour
 the frog's eyes
   —open

That moment at dusk
when birds stop singing.

             on the river
                  a cloud
moves faster than it moves

rings as they move
through ripples—
caterpillar

hanging
from a cliff—
           roots of a tree

on the lake
          loons listening
          `to loons

   High tide:
shifting of stones
   on the floor
   of the sea.

caught
       in crooked icicles—
         the wind

Epilogue

Voices of frogs
As if to accompany
All those stars
        —Eleanor Wolff

Sources and Credits for One Hundred Frogs, I

Aitken, Robert. *Blind Donkey*, 1 (1975): 1–2. Reprinted with permission.

———. *A Zen Wave: Bashō's Haiku & Zen*. Tokyo: John Weatherhill, 1978. Reprinted with permission.

Akimoto, Shunkichi. *Exploring the Japanese Ways of Life*. Tokyo: Tokyo News Service, 1961. Reprinted with permission.

Alexander, Scott. *Haiku West* 1, no. 1 (June 1967). Attempts to get in touch with the author were futile.

Anonymous. "Haiku and the West . . . ," *The Times Educational Supplement*, March 20, 1959. Reprinted with permission of Times Newspapers.

Anonymous. *Don't Tell the Scarecrow*. New York: Scholastic Book Services, 1969. Attempts to identify the translator were fruitless. Reprinted with permission of the publisher.

Aston, W. G. *A History of Japanese Literature*. New York: D. Appleton Century, 1899.

Behn, Harry. *Cricket Songs: Japanese Haiku*. New York: Harcourt Brace Jovanovich, 1964. Reprinted with permission.

Beilenson, Peter. *Japanese Haiku*. Mount Vernon, New York: Peter Pauper Press, 1956. Reprinted with permission. A version with the same wording, but arranged in three lines and aligned at left, appears in his *Lotus Blossoms* (New York: Peter Pauper Press, 1970).

Beilenson, Peter, and Behn, Harry. *Haiku Harvest*. Mount Vernon, New York: Peter Pauper Press, 1962. Reprinted with permission.

Blyth, R. H. *Zen in English Literature and Oriental Classics*. Tokyo: Hokuseido Press, 1942. Reprinted with permission.

————. *Haiku,* vol 1. Tokyo: Hokuseido Press, 1949. Reprinted with permission.

Bond, Edward. *Narrow Road to the Deep North.* New York: Hill & Wang, 1969. Reprinted with permission of Farrar, Strauss & Giroux.

Bownas, Geoffrey, and Thwaite, Anthony. *The Penguin Book of Japanese Verse.* Harmondsworth, Middlesex: Penguin Books, 1964. © Geoffrey Bownas and Anthony Thwaite. Reprinted with permission.

Britton, Dorothy. *A Haiku Journey: Bashō's "The Narrow Road to the Far North" and Selected Haiku.* Tokyo: Kodansha International, 1974. Reprinted with permission.

Brower, Robert H. "Japanese," *Versification: Major Language Types.* Edited by W. K. Wimsatt. New York: New York University Press, 1972. Reprinted with permission.

Bryan, John Thomas. *The Literature of Japan.* New York: Kennikat Press, 1929. Attempts to get permission were fruitless.

Buchanan, Daniel C. *One Hundred Famous Haiku.* San Francisco: Japan Publications, 1973. Attempts to get permission were fruitless.

Cassedy, Sylvia, and Kunihiro, Suetake. *Birds, Frogs, and Moonlight.* New York: Doubleday & Co., 1967. Reprinted with permission.

Chamberlain, Basil Hall. "Bashō and the Japanese Poetical Epigram," *Transactions of the Asiatic Society of Japan* 30, no. 2 (1902). From the typographical arrangement, Chamberlain seems to have intended this as a "literal" translation, rather than a "poetic" one.

Cohen, William Howard. *To Walk in Seasons.* Tokyo: Charles E. Tuttle Co., 1972. Reprinted with permission.

Corman, Cid. *Cool Gong.* Ashland, Massachusetts: Origin Press, 1959. Reprinted with permission.

Emerson, Gertrude. "Haikai Poetry," *The Forum* 51 (March 1914).

Fraser, G. S. "The Frog and the Pond: First Steps in Japanese Poetics," *Nine* 3, no. 4, whole no. 9 (Summer–Autumn 1952). Attempts to get permission were futile.

————. *Metre, Rhyme and Free Verse.* London: Methuen, 1970. Attempts to get permission led nowhere.

Ginsberg, Allen. *The New York Times,* February 16, 1979. Ginsberg has a poem of fourteen quatrains, *Old Pond,* beginning with the line, "The old pond—a frog jumps in, kerplunk!" in *Zero* 2 (1979).

Giroux, Joan. *The Haiku Form.* Tokyo: Charles E. Tuttle Co., 1974. Reprinted with permission.

Hearn, Lafcadio. *Exotics and Retrospectives in Ghostly Japan*. Boston: Little, Brown & Co. 1898. In the Charles E. Tuttle Co. reprint of the book, the translation appears as "Old pond—frogs jumping in—sound of water."

Henderson, Harold G. "Haiku—Ancient and Modern," *Asia* 24 (February 1934).

———. *An Introduction to Haiku*. New York: Doubleday & Co., 1958. Reprinted with permission.

Higginson, William J. *Itadakimasu*. Kanona, New York: J & C Transcripts, 1971. Reprinted with permission.

Ibanez, Felix-Marti. "The Time Talisman," *Chanoyu Quarterly*, no. 13 (1976). Reprinted with permission of the Urasenke Foundation.

Ikeda, Kenjun. "English haiku no mondai-ten," *Minerva*, no. 2 (1972). Attempts to get permission were futile.

Janeira, Armando Martins. *Japanese and Western Literature*. Tokyo: Charles E. Tuttle Co., 1970. Reprinted with permission.

Keene, Donald. *Japanese Literature: An Introduction for Western Readers*. New York: Grove Press, 1955. Reprinted with permission. The second version appears in three lines, aligned at left and with a slight typographical variation, in his *World Within Walls* (New York: Holt, Rinehart & Winston, 1976).

Maeda, Cana. "On Translating the *Haiku* Form," *Harvard Journal of Asiatic Studies* 29 (1969). Reprinted with permission of the editors of the *Journal*.

Marks, Alfred H. "Haiku in Japanese and English," *Chanoyu Quarterly*, no. 9 (1974). Reprinted with permission of the Urasenke Foundation.

Masaoka, Shiki. *Shiki Zenshū*, vol. 4. Tokyo: Kodansha, 1978. This translation appears in Shiki's college paper in English, "Baseo as a Poet," which is thought to have been written in 1892.

Miner, Earl. *Japanese Linked Poetry*. Princeton: Princeton University Press, 1979. Reprinted with permission.

Miner, Earl, and Odagiri, Hiroko. *The Monkey's Straw Raincoat*. Princeton: Princeton University Press, 1981. Reprinted with permission.

Miyamori, Asataro. *One Thousand Haiku Ancient and Modern*. Tokyo: Dobunsha, 1930.

———. *An Anthology of Haiku Ancient and Modern*. Tokyo: Maruzen, 1932.

Nippon Gakujutsu Shinkōkai. *Haikai and Haiku*. Tokyo: Nippon Gakujutsu Shinkōkai, 1958. Reprinted with permission.

Nitobe, Inazo. *Japanese Traits and Foreign Influences*. London: Trubner, 1927.

———. *Lectures on Japan*. Tokyo: Kenkyusha, 1936.

Noguchi, Yone. *The Spirit of Japanese Poetry*. London: John Murray, 1914.

O'Donnol, Dion. "One sheet (green) printing of 'the frog poem' as used in my poetry classes in the 1963–1969 period" (as described by the author). Reprinted with author's permission.

———. "Splash, Classical Japanese Haiku, Englished by Dion O'Donnol" (1968). Reprinted with author's permission.

Otake, Masaru V. "The Haiku Touch in Wallace Stevens and Some Imagists," *East-West Review* 2, no. 2 (Winter 1965–66). Reprinted with permission.

Page, Curtis Hidden. *Japanese Poetry, an historical essay*. Boston: Houghton Mifflin, 1923. Reprinted with permission of the Estate of Curtis Hidden Page.

Porter, William J. *A Year of Japanese Epigrams*. London: Oxford University Press, 1911. Reprinted with permission.

Rexroth, Kenneth. *One Hundred Poems from the Japanese*. New York: New Directions, 1955. Reprinted with permission.

Saisho, Fumiko. "A Few Notes on 'Haikai' and the Japanese Mind," *Cultural Nippon* 3, no. 2 (June 1935). Attempts to get permission led nowhere.

Saito, Hidesaburo. As cited in Miyamori's *Anthology* (which see).

Seidensticker, Edward G., and Nasu, Kiyoshi. *Nihongo-rashii Hyōgen kara Eigo-rashii Hyōgen e*. Tokyo: Baifūkan, 1962. Reprinted with permission.

Stewart, Harold. *A Net of Fireflies*. Tokyo: Charles E. Tuttle Co., 1960. Reprinted with permission.

Stryk, Lucien, and Ikemoto, Takashi. *Haiku of the Japanese Masters*. Derry, Pennsylvania: The Rook Press, 1977. The translation also appears in *The Penguin Book of Zen Poetry* (New York: Viking/Penguin, 1981). Reprinted with permission.

Suzuki, Daisetz T. "Zen and Japanese Poetry," *Contemporary Japan* 10, no. 4 (April 1941).

———. *Zen and Japanese Culture*. Princeton: Princeton University Press, 1959. Reprinted with permission.

Takamine, Hiroshi. "Love and Haiku," *Today's Japan* 13, no. 9 (September 1958). Attempts to get permission led nowhere.

Toyoda, Minoru. As cited in Miyamori's *Anthology* (which see).

Ueda, Makoto. *Matsuo Bashō*. New York: Twayne Publishers, 1970. Reprinted with permission of G. K. Hall.

Walsh, Clara A. *The Master-Singers of Japan*. London: John Murray, 1910.

Yasuda, Kenneth. *A Pepper Pod*. New York: Alfred A. Knopf, 1947. Reprinted with permission of Charles E. Tuttle Co.

Yuasa, Nobuyuki. *Basho: The Narrow Road to the Deep North and Other Travel Sketches*. Harmondsworth, Middlesex: Penguin Books, 1966. © Nobuyuki Yuasa. Reprinted with permission.

Index

Those who appear only by their personal
names in the text are so identified here.

acrostic, 35–36
ageku (ending part), 31, 106
Aitken, Robert, 163, 164; *A Zen Wave,* 130
Akao Tōshi (born 1925), 123
Akimoto, Shunkichi, 157
Alexander, Scott, 159
Amann, Eric, *The Wordless Poem: A Study of Zen,* 129
Ameyama Minoru (born 1926), 125
Arakida Moritake (1473–1549), 73; on diction, 56; *Tobiume Senku* (Flying Plum: Thousand Pieces), 50–52, 55–59
Asakarishū (Hemp-Gathering Collection), 110; see also *waki-okoshi*
Asō Isoji, 110
Aston, W. G., 151

Baken, 85
Bashō, *see* Matsuo Bashō

Bashō school, 113; see also *Shōfū*
Behn, Harry, 157, 158
Beilenson, Peter, 155, 157
Blyth, R. H., 129, 154
Bonchō, *see* Nozawa Bonchō
Bond, Edward, 160
Bontō (1349–1420?), 46
Bōsui, 86
Botange Shōhaku (1443–1527), 51; renga by, 46–50
Bownas, Geoffrey, 158
Britton, Dorothy, 161
Brower, Robert H., 161
Bryan, John Thomas, 152
Buchanan, Daniel C., 161

Cassedy, Sylvia, 159
Chamberlain, Basil Hall, 126, 129, 130, 151
Chikuba Kyōginshū (Collection of Mad Songs Made on Bamboo Stilts), 51

Chiyojo (1703–75), 119
chōka (long song), 6, 8
Chuang Tzu, 53, 76, 77
Cicada, 179
Cohen, William Howard, 161
Corman, Cid, 156

daisan (third part), 31, 58, 71
Danno, Yoko, 165
Danrin (school), 59, 65, 113; and Bashō, 70–71, 74; and *Furuike ya,* 149
Davidson, L. A., 182, 208–9
Deemer, Bill, 165

Einbond, Bernard Lionel, 165
Eiun, 38, 40, 41
Emerson, Gertude, 152
Enokoshū (Puppy's Collection), 113–14
Etsujin, *see* Ochi Etsujin

Fagan, Robert Anthony, 166
Farewell Gift to Sora, A, (*Sora Sen*), 82, 93–106
Figgins, Ross, 150, 166
Flygare, Wᵐ, 167–68
Fraser, G. S., 154–55, 160
Frogpond, 179
fūga, see *fūryū*
Fujita Shōshi (born 1926), 125
Fujiwara no Ietada (14th century), 41
Fujiwara no Ietaka (1158–1237), 16
Fujiwara no Kiyosuke (1104–77), 48–49
Fujiwara no Mototoshi (died 1142), 50

Fujiwara no Sanesada (1130–91), 73
Fujiwara no Shunzei (1114–1204), 46
Fujiwara no Tameuji (1222–86), 52
Fujiwara no Tameyo (1251–1338), 43–44
Fujiwara no Teika (1162–1241), 13–15, 17, 28, 34, 46; on allusion, 23; *Eiga Taigai* (Outline for Composing Tanka), 23; *Meigetsuki* (Diary of the Bright Moon), 13–14; *tsukeai* by, 15
Fujiwara no Yukiie (dates uncertain), 48
Fukui Kyūzō (1867–1951), 4–6, 46
fūkyō, see *fūryū*
Furuike ya, see Matsuo Bashō
fūryū (eccentricity, poetic dementia), 22, 77–78, 110, 118
fushimono (incorporated object), 14–16, 33–35, 47
Fuyu no Hi (Winter Day), 79, 82

Ginsburg, Allen, 164
Giroux, Joan, 162; *The Haiku Form,* 129
Glandon, Clyde C., 207
Gotoba, retired emperor (1180–1239), 8–9, 28; and early *renga,* 12–17; *tanka* by, 9, 46; *tsukeai* by, 16
Gusai, monk (1282–1376), 17, 31; *renga* by, 36–42; *tsukeai* by, 25–26
Gyōa, 39

haibun (haikai prose), 74–75, 110

haijin (haiku poet), 127

haikai (humor), 43, 50–61, 63, 67, 116, 117, 135; diction, 55–56; see also *haikai no renga*

haikai no makoto (essence of haikai), 81

haikai no renga (humorous renga), 50–51; decline of, 106–112; and Noh, 72; rules, 59

haiku (haikai part), 3; in English, 207–21, 223; *haijin*, 127; question on, 126–131; lineation of, 136–44; and Masaoka Shiki, 30; Scholarly treatment of, in English, 126–27; and Taoism, 77–78; translation of, 135–43; and Zen, 129–31

Haiku Anthology, 127, 129

Haiku Magazine, 179

Haiku Society of America, 126, 136, 179, 207

Haiku Society of Canada, 126, 179

Hanzan, 84

Hara Sekitei (1886–1951), 122

Harr, Lorraine Ellis, 168–69

Hashimoto Takako (1899–1963), 123

Hattori Tohō (1657–1730), 116, 149; on *Furuike ya*, 81; on *fūryū*, 78; *hokku* by, 119; *Sanzōshi* (Three Booklets), 128

Hayashi Tōyō (died 1712), 80, 83

Hearn, Lafcadio, 151

Hekigodō, *see* Kawahigashi Hekigodō

Henderson, Harold G., 153, 155–56; *An Introduction to Haiku*, 129

Higginson, William J., 150, 161, 181

hikichigae (contrariness), 21–22

hirazuke (straight linking), 18–19

Hōjin, 86

hokku (opening part), 54, 58, 61–63, 65–66, 71, 72; allusion, 46, 72–74, 76; definition, 29, 113, 114, 128–29; *Furuike ya*, 81–82, *see also* Matsuo Bashō; *fūryū* in, 78; *fushimono*, 34–35, 37, 47; with *haibun*, 74–77; *ji-hokku*, 117; and *renga*, 111; solecistic, 79–80; *tateku*, 117; transition to haiku, 113–18; translation of, 135; with *waki*, 79–80, 85, 90, 91–93, 149

Hokushi, *see* Tachibana Hokushi

hon'i (true import), 67

honka (allusion to a tanka), 23

honzetsu (allusion to a well-known story, anecdote, or Chinese poem), 23

Hototogisu (Cuckoo), 139

Hubbell, Lindley Williams, 169, 203–6

Ibanez, Felix-Marti, 163

Ichijō Kanera (1402–81), 35

Ichiryū, 83

Ichū, *see* Okanishi Ichū

Ii, 85

Iida Atsuoi (died 1826), 120

Iida Dakotsu (1885–1962), 121

Iida Ryūta (born 1920), 124

Iio Sōgi (1421–1502), 28; *renga* by, 46–50; *tsukeai* by, 51

Ikeda, Kenjun, 161

Ikemoto, Takeshi, 163

imagism, 72–73, 126–27

Impumon-in no Taifu (12th century), 48

Inen, 87

Inu Tsukubashū (Dog's Tsukuba Collection), 51–52, 58; quoted from 52–55, 60, 108

Isaacson, Harold J., *Peonies Kana: Haiku by the Upasaka Shiki*, 147

Ishida Hakyō (born 1912), 122

Ishihara Yatsuka (born 1919), 124

Issa, *see* Kobayashi Issa

Itō Shintoku (1633–98), 71–72

Janeira, Armando Martins, 160

jiyu-ritsu (free rhythm) haiku, 137

jo-ha-kyū (introduction, elaboration, finale), 26–27, 40

Jōsō, *see* Naitō Jōsō

Jūgo, 77

Juntoku, emperor (1197–1242), *Yakumo Mishō* (Some Thoughts on Yakumo), 17

Jūshin, 82

Kaai Sora (1649–1710), 92; *hokku* by, 93; *renga* by, 94–100; *tsukeai* by, 83

Kabashira (A Column of Mosquitos), 65–71

Kadokawa Gen'yoshi (1917–75), 124

Kagami Shikō (1665–1731): *Kuzu no Matsubara* (Pine Grove with Kudzu), 149; *tsukeai* by, 84, 86, 87; *waki* by, 116

Kai (Oars) Group, 112, 180

Kai: Renshi, 112

kajin (tanka poet), 127–28

Kakei, 76, 79–80

kakushi-dai (hidden topic), 22–23

Kanaseki, Hisao, 169

Kaneko Tōta (born 1919), 124

Kanokobata Suitō (born 1663), 91

Karai Senryū (1718–90), 108

kasen (divine poet), 80, 82, 91, 92, 179

Kasen, 112

Kasshin, 83

katauta (half song), 8

Katō Kyōtai (1732–92), 120

Katō Shūson (born 1905), 122

Katsura Nobuko (born 1914), 124

Kawahigashi Hekigodō (1873–1937), 121, 138

Kawazu Awase (Frog Matches), 148

Kaya Shirao (1738?–91), 120

Keene, Donald, 155

keiki (landscape), 19

kigo (seasonal word), 30, 94, 108, 135

Kikaku, *see* Takarai Kikaku

Ki no Tsurayuki (c. 868–c. 946), 62–63

Kin'yōshū (Collection of Gold-Leafed Poems), 12, 48

kireji (cutting word), 47, 147

Kirkup, James, 170, 184, 189–92

Kisen, 83

Kishida Chigyo (born 1918), 124

Kitsuda Shunko (1815–86), *Bashō-ō Furuike Shinden* (A True History of the Venerable Bashō's Old Pond), 149–50

Kobayashi Issa (1763–1827), 117–18, 120

Kōbunta, 4, 7

Kojiki (Record of Ancient Matters), 7, 9, 103

Kokinshū (Collection of Ancient and Modern Poems), 29, 47, 81, 116

kokoro-zuke (linking "by heart"), 19, 64–71

Komparu Zenchiku (1405–68), *Senju,* 58

Kondō Tadashi, 150, 185

Kōtan, 80

kotoba-zuke (linking by word), 20, 22, 61–65

Kuenstler, Frank, 170

Kusama Tokihiko (born 1920), 124

Kyokusui, 84

Kyorai, *see* Mukai Kyorai

Kyoshi, *see* Takahama Kyoshi

Lamb, Elizabeth Searle, 181, 182, 210–11

lien-chü (Chinese linked poetry), 11

Little, Geraldine C., 195–98, 212

Maeda, Cana, 160

maeku (preceding part), 53, 108–9

maeku-zuke (linking to a preceding part), 24, 108–9

Man'yōshū (Collection of Ten Thousand Leaves), 6, 7, 8, 9, 103

Marks, Alfred, 162–63; "Haiku in Japanese and English," 207

Masaoka Shiki (1867–1902), 137–40, 142, 151; on *Furuike ya,* 147; haiku (term), 30; haiku by, 121, 137; on *renga,* 111; transition from *hokku* to haiku, 110–12, 113–14, 118

Matheson, William, 170–72, 183, 186–87

Matsunaga Teitoku (1571–1653), 59–64, 71; on linking, 60–64; morality, 59–61; *renga* by, 61–64; *Shinzō Inu Tsukubashū* (New and Enlarged Dog's Tsukuba Collection), 60–61; *Tensui Shō* (Heavenly Water), 61; *tsukeai* by, 60–61; *Uta Izure* (Which Sings Better), 61–64

Matsuo-Allard, R. Clarence, 172

Matsuo Bashō (1644–94), 3, 18, 23, 27, 59, 71–87, 106,

108, 127, 136, 148; and
Chinese poetry, 75–76; on
conduct, 90, 102; on Dan-
rin, 74; *A Farewell Gift to
Sora,* 82, 93–106; *Furuike
ya,* 81–82, 118, 149 (dif-
ferent version, 149; expli-
cation of, 147–48; referred
to, 130, 147; translations of,
151–75; with *waki,* 149); on
fūryū, 78; *haibun* by, 74–75,
93; on *haikai,* 114; on *hokku,*
128–29; *hokku* by, 63, 71–72,
73, 74, 75, 76, 78–81, 91–93,
114–15, 118, 128, 131; inde-
pendence, 108; journey to
the north, 91–94; *Kai Oi*
(Shell Matches), 114; *karumi*
(lightness), 95; and language,
29, 43; "moon and flower,"
31–32; name, 54; *Nozarashi
Kikō* (Skull-Exposed-in-a-Field
Diary), 76; *Oku no Hoso-
michi* (The Narrow Road to
the Interior), 91–94, 110;
on poetics, 82, 106; *renga* by
71–72, 77, 94–106; *renga* ses-
sion, 88–91; scholarship on,
108, 110; on sequential devel-
opment, 27; and Sōin, 59–
60; as a *sōshō,* 74, 106; style
of, 79; and Taoist philos-
ophy, 77–78; *tsukeai* by, 79,
82–87; and Zen, 131

McClintock, Michael, 181,
182–84

Meredith, Philip, 185

Minamoto no Nakatsuna (12th
century), 104

Minamoto no Shigeyuki (died
1000), 3–4, 7

Minamoto no Toshiyori (1055–
1129), 3–4; on linking, 12;
Samboku Kikashū (Collection
of a Do-Nothing's Eccentric
Poems), 12; *Zuinō* (Elemental
Poetics), 3, 11, 12

Minamoto no Yorimasa (1104–
80), 68

Miner, Earl, 145–46, 164; *Japa-
nese Linked Poetry,* 146

Mitsuhashi Takajo (1899–1972),
123

Miyamori, Asataro, 152–53

Miyake Shōzan (1718–1801),
119

Miyazaki Sensen (died 1706),
84, 95

Mizuhara Shūōshi (born 1892),
122, 140

Mokuchin, 39

moon and flower, 31–32, 38,
110–12; positions of, 32

Morimoto Norio (born 1917),
142–43

Moritake, *see* Arakida Mori-
take

Mukai Kyorai (1651–1704),
149; *hokku* by, 78, 118, 148;
on *hokku,* 116; *renga* by, 144;
on *renga* sessions, 89; on se-
quential development, 27;
tsukeai by, 82, 84

mumon (solids or ground), 28

Murakami Kijō (1865–1938),
121

mushin ("mind-lacking," or non-
professional), 13

nadokoro (famous places), 23

Naitō Jōsō (1662–1704), 86, 119

Nakamura Kusatao (born 1901), 122

Nakamura Fumikuni (17th century), 144

Nakatsukasa Ippekirō (1887–1946), 121

Natsume Seibi (1749–1816), 120

Nihon Shoki (History of Japan), 10

Nijō Yoshimoto (1320–88), 31, 50, 106–7; diction, 29; on attitude toward *renga,* 44–46; on *fushimono,* 35; on *hokku,* 29; *kigo,* list of, by, 30; on linking, 23; on origin of *renga,* 10–11; on quality of each part, 27–28; renga by, 36–42; on *renga* sessions, 89; rules, 17–36; on sequential development, 26; *Tsukuba Mondō* (Questions and Answers on Tsukuba), 11; *tsukeai* by, 24; on *wakiku,* 31

Nikt, Clare, 172

Nippon (Japan), 138, 139

Nishiyama Sōin (1605–82), 59–60; linking of, 64–71; *renga* by, 65–70

Nitobe, Inazo, 152, 154

Noguchi, Yone, 152

Nōin, monk (born 988), 105

Nomiyama Asuka (1917–70), 123

Nozawa Bonchō (died 1714), 84, 144

Nozawa Setsuko (born 1920), 125

O'Brien, Geoffrey, 187–92

O'Brien, Michael, 173, 186–88, 203–6

Ochi Etsujin (1656–1739), 83, 119

O'Donnol, Dion, 158, 159

Ōe Shigekazu (14th century), 39–41

Ogiwara Seisensui (1884–1976), 121, 138–39; *Sōun* (Strati), 138

Okanishi Ichū (1639–1711), 65–70; *Haikai Mōgyū* (Haikai Meng Ch'iu), 66; *Shibu Uchiwa Hentō* (Response to A Conservative's Fan), 65

Oku no Hosomichi (The Narrow Road to the Interior), *see* Matsuo Bashō

Onishi, Sakura, 185

Otake, Masaru V., 158

Ōtomo no Yakamochi (716–85?), 6, 8

Owen, Maureen, 173

Ozaki Hōsai (1885–1926), 121, 138–39

Padget, Ron, 173

Page, Curtis Hidden, 152, 169

palindrome, 36

Patterson, Cyril, 173–74

Pauly, Bill, 182

Paz, Octavio, et al., *Renga: A Chain of Poems,* 180

Po Chü-yi (772–846), 11, 21, 74–75

Porter, William J., 151

Poulter, S. L., 182–83
Pound, Ezra, 72–73, 130
Rashburn, Jody, 185
renga (linked poetry), 3; allusion, 72–74; and Bashō, 88; diction, 29; "disjunctive linking" (Earl Miner's phrase), 3, 112, 179; in English, 179–206 (format, 180; rules, 179–80; times and means, 180); form, 18; and *hokku*, 88; illustrative anecdotes, 3–6; intensity of linking, 28–29; length, 13–14, 17, 18; linking, 3, 13, 18–24, 97, 112, 179; "moon and flower," 31–32; orthodox *renga*, 59, 66; quality of each part, 27–28; relation to *tanka*, 6, 7–9, 43; rules, 18–36; sequential development, 26–27; session, 88–90; subject categories, 16–17; translation of, 143–46; wit and humor, 43, 108
Renga: A Chain of Poems, see Paz, Octavio
Rexroth, Kenneth, 155
rinne (samsara or recurrence), 34
Rōka, 86
Roseliep, Raymond, 213–15
Roten, 85
Ruch, Barbara, 174

sabi (elegance in deprivation), 100
Sagara Tōkyū (1638–1715), 91–92

Saiokuken Sōchō (1448–1532), 46–49, 51
Saisho, Fumiko, 153
Saito, Hidesaburo, 153
Saitō Sani (1900–1962), 123
Saitō Tokugen (1559–1647), *Haikai Shogaku Shō* (Haikai Primer), 56
Sakagami Kōshun (1649–1707), 116
Sakurai Baishitsu (1769–1852), 120
Sampū, *see* Sugiyama Sampū
Sanjō, emperor (976–1017), 67
Santen, 85
Sato, Hiroaki, 183, 184, 186–92, 195–206
Satō Onifusa (born 1919), 124
Satomura Jōha (1524–1602), 59, 99
Sawaki Kin'ichi (born 1919), 125
Seidensticker, Edward G., 157
Seifū, 84
Seisensui, *see* Ogiwara Seisensui
Selden, Kyoko, 147, 184–85, 186–87
Senka (17th century), 148
senryū, 108–9; translation of, 136–37; *see also* Karai Senryū
Sensen, *see* Miyazaki Sensen
Senzaishū (Collection of Poems for a Thousand Generations), 48–49, 50, 73
Sequence Revised by Bashō (*Okina Naoshi no Maki*), see *Farewell Gift to Sora, A*
Shadō, 84
Shibu Uchiwa (A Conservative's Fan), 65

Shifū, 82

Shigenobu, *see* Takayanagi Shigenobu

Shigeyuki, *see* Minamoto no Shigeyuki

shijin (poet), 127

Shiki, *see* Masaoka Shiki

shikimoku (rules), 32–34

Shikō, *see* Kagami Shikō

Shinkei, monk (1406–75): on attitude toward *renga*, 44–46; on linking, 28–29

Shin Kokinshū (New Collection of Ancient and Modern Poems), 8–9, 12–13, 23, 48, 49, 105

Shinohara Bon (born 1910), 123

Shinsen Tsukubashū (New Tsukuba Collection), 50, 52

Shita Yaba (1663–1740), 78, 85

Shōfū (Bashō style), 79–82; definition, 79

Shōhaku, *see* Botange Shōhaku

Shōtetsu (1381–1459), 36

Shūa, 38, 40–41

shūhitsu (scribe), 88–89

Shūishū (Collection of Gleaned Poems), 29, 62–63

Soa, 38, 40

Sōchō, *see* Saiokuken Sōchō

Sōgi, *see* Iio Sōgi

Sōin, *see* Nishiyama Sōin

Sōkan, *see* Yamazaki Sōkan

Sora, *see* Kaai Sora

sōshō (master), 74, 88–89, 106–8

sōtai (contrast), 21

Sōzei, *see* Takayama Sōzei

Stewart, Harold, 157

Stryk, Lucien, 163

Suetake, Kunihiro, 158

Sugawara no Michizane (845–903), 30, 56–57, 89

Sugita Hisajo (1890–1946), 122

Sugiyama Sampū (1647–1732), 85, 119, 148

Sukan, 83

Suzuki, Daisetz T., 154, 157; on haiku, 130–31; "Zen and Haiku," 130

Suzuki Murio (born 1919), 125

Tachibana Hokushi (died 1718), 94–106

Tagawa Hōrō (1726–1845), 120

Tagawa Hiryoshi (born 1914), 125

Taisui, 85

Takahama Kyoshi (1874–1959), 121, 138, 139–40

Takakuwa Rankō (1726–98), 120

Takamine, Hiroshi, 156

Takamura Kōtarō (1883–1956), 130

Takarai Kikaku (1661–1707), 118, 135, 149

Takayama Sōzei (died 1455), 35–36, 52

Takayanagi Shigenobu (born 1923), 140–42, 143

Tale of Genji, The, 14, 21, 29

Tale of the Heike, The, 58, 104

Tales of Ise, 9, 29

Tamemasa, governor of Kawachi, 3–4, 7

Taneda Santōka (1882–1940), 123, 139

Tani Sōboku (1488?–1545), 26–27

tanka (short song), 6, 7, 8; change in syllabic break, 8–9; source of allusion, 23, 73–74; tanka form used in *renga*, 79; tanka poet, 127–28

tanshi (short poem), 137

tanshō (short piece), 137

Tan Taigi (1709–71), 119

Taoist philosophy, 77; see also *Chuang Tzu*

Teika, *see* Fujiwara no Teika

Teimon (school), 59, 64–65

Teitoku, *see* Matsunaga Teitoku

Tempō, 85

Tennyson, Alfred, *Tithonus,* 73

Three Poets at Minase, 9, 46–50

Thwaite, Anthony, 158

Tobi no Ha mo (A Kite's Feathers, Too), 144–46

Tobiume Senku (Flying Plum: Thousand Pieces), *see* Arakida Moritake

Tohō, *see* Hattori Tohō

Tokoku, 79

Tokugawa shogunate, 59, 107

Tomizawa Kakio (1902–62), 123, 140

Tomohira, prince (964–1009), 49

Toshiyori, *see* Minamoto no Toshiyori

Tōyō, see Hayashi Tōyō

Toyoda, Minoru, 153

tsukeai (linking together), 24, 52, 108

tsukeku (linked part), 55, 60, 63, 108

Tsukubashū (Tsukuba Collection), 10, 17, 24, 50, 113; quoted from, 16, 21, 22, 24–26, 30, 52; *see also* Gusai, Nijō Yoshimoto

Tsurayuki, *see* Ki no Tsurayuki

Tu Fu (712–70), 75

Ueda, Makoto, 160

umon (prints or design), 28

uta-awase (tanka matches), 9–10

ushin ("mind-possessing," or professional), 13

uzumi-ku (buried allusion), 20–21

van den Heuvel, Cor: on English haiku, 127; haiku by, 216–17; *The Haiku Anthology,* 127, 129; *renga* by, 183–84, 193–94 *senryū* by, 217

waki, wakiku (accompanying part), 31, 71, 72, 80

waki-okoshi (practice in which a renga sequence was begun with a hokku of a famous poet of the past), 110

Walsh, Clara A., 151

Western World Haiku Society, 126

Wills, John, 183–84

Wills, Marlene, haiku by, 207, 218–20; *renga* by, 182, 186, 195–98

Wolfe, Stephen, 207

Wolff, Eleanor, 150, 175–223
Wordsworth, William, *Lyrical Ballads*, 59

Yaba, *see* Shita Yaba
Yamaguchi Seishi (born 1901), 122
Yamaguchi Seison (born 1892), 122
Yamaguchi Sodō (also Shinshō, 1642–1716), 71–72
Yamamoto Kenkichi (born 1907), 128–29, 149
Yamato, empress (7th century), 8
Yamazaki Sōkan (died c. 1550), 51–52, 58–59, 60
yariku (quick part), 103
Yasuda, Kenneth, 154; *The Japanese Haiku*, 129
Yasui, 77
Yosa Buson (1716–83), *hokku* by, 78, 117, 119

yosei (overtone), 21
Yoshida Kenkō (1282–1350), *Tsurezuregusa* (Essays in Idleness), 66
Yoshimoto, *see* Nijō Yoshimoto
yotsude (two for two), 19
Young, George M., Jr., 175
Young, Kristine, 185
Young, Virginia Brady, 182–83, 221
yoyoshi (44-part sequence), 107
Yuasa, Nobuyuki, 159
yūgen (subdued elegance), 10
Yūgiku, 83

Zen, 129–31, 148, 150
Zenrin Kushū (A Zen Phrase Anthology), 73
Zuinō (Elemental Poetics), 3, 11, 12; *see also* Minamoto no Toshiyori

The "weathermark" identifies this book as a production of John Weatherhill, Inc., publishers of fine books on Asia and the Pacific. Book Design and typography: Meredith Weatherby and Miriam F. Yamaguchi. Layout of illustrations: Yutaka Shimoji. Composition of the text: Samhwa Printing Co., Seoul. Printing of the text: Kenkyusha Printing Co., Tokyo. Engraving and printing of the plates, in monochrome offset: Kinmei Printing Co., Tokyo. Binding: Makoto Binderies, Tokyo. The typeface used in the text is Monotype Perpetua with hand-set Optima for display.